Pelican Books

Understanding the Female Orgasm

Understanding the Female Orgasm

Seymour
Fisher

Penguin
Books

Penguin Books Ltd, Harmondsworth
Middlesex, England
Penguin Books, 625 Madison Avenue,
New York, New York 10022, U.S.A.
Penguin Books Australia Ltd, Ringwood,
Victoria, Australia
Penguin Books Canada Ltd, 2801 John Street,
Markham, Ontario, Canada
Penguin Books (N.Z.) Ltd,
182–190 Wairau Road,
Auckland 10, New Zealand

First published in the U.S.A. by Basic Books 1973
First published in Great Britain in Pelican Books 1973
Reprinted 1975, 1977

Made and printed in Great Britain by
Hazell Watson & Viney Ltd, Aylesbury, Bucks
Set in Linotype Juliana

Contents

Preface

My intention in this book is to spell out what we know about sexual behaviour and sexual responsiveness in women. The material presented is a condensed version of my larger scientific study (*The Female Orgasm: Psychology, Physiology, Fantasy*, Allen Lane, 1973) dealing with female sexuality. *The Female Orgasm* sought to provide a thorough analysis of all scientific literature dealing with sexual responsiveness in women and also described a series of studies undertaken in my laboratory at the Upstate Medical Center in Syracuse, New York, to determine the factors governing a woman's ability to attain orgasm. The studies involved middle-class women whose sexual feelings and fantasies were minutely examined.

My scientific interest in sexuality developed logically out of my previous research. I had devoted many years to the study of how the individual experiences his body psychologically, exploring such areas as how the child learns to make sense of his body; how the adolescent copes with the enormous alterations in his body structure; and how the amputee adjusts to the loss of his body substance. In the process of investigating body feelings, it is inevitable that questions will arise about primary appetites like hunger and sexual excitement, which so often dominate the world of the body. My initial research with sexual behaviour was therefore concerned with understanding the role of sexuality in the average person's view of his own body. As I began to look at what was scientifically known about sexual response in humans, especially at the psychological level, I was struck by three things. First, there were many contending and often contradictory theories about the determinants of sexual responsiveness. Second, little if any scientific work had been done to test these theories. Third, it was sadly true that despite the absence of scientific data, the proponents of each theory vehemently asserted its validity and denied the reasonableness of other theories. Perhaps even more sadly, I observed that on the basis of largely untested assumptions many so-called 'sex experts' were pouring forth streams of advice to the world about how normal people should feel and behave sexually. Even highly trained professional counsellors and psychotherapists were advising people that they were 'sick' or maladjusted because they did not conform to hypothetical models of 'mature sexuality'. For example, many women had been burdened with the obligation to enter into psychoanalytic treatment because they could not attain the so-called 'vaginal orgasm'. They had been told that achieving orgasm primarily through direct clitoral stimulation was a sign of immaturity and even serious psychological maladjustment. I could find no scientific support for this dogma which was endlessly repeated. It was from this perspective that I became increasingly interested in understanding human sexual experience.

I turned particularly to studying sexuality in women because the greatest confusion and disagreement seems to exist in this realm. One primary step that I took was to collect and analyse the entire existing scientific literature dealing with female sexual response. I tried to do so with a minimum of prejudice – simply looking over all the data to see what would crystallize out as true or untrue. It became increasingly clear that few if any of the existing theories concerning female sexuality could sensibly embrace the empirical facts. Subsequently, I undertook a series of studies (extending over a five-year period, 1965–70) concerned with providing a more exact and durable model of female sexual response. These studies were at first exploratory and not guided by specific hypotheses. But as they uncovered new information they became more exact and concerned with answering specific questions. In the pages that follow I will relate the course we took in our attempts to understand the sexual behaviour of women.

The women we studied were asked to provide information about many different aspects of their sexual feelings and practices. Inquiries were made about such matters as the following: techniques by which orgasm is attained; feelings during and after orgasm; preferences for clitoral versus vaginal stimulation; foreplay practices; intensity of orgasm; intercourse conditions favouring achievement of orgasm; fantasies and images occurring during sexual arousal; vaginal, clitoral, and breast sensations; intercourse frequency; enjoyment of masturbation; and the manner in which sex information was originally acquired. Special efforts were made to ascertain how each woman experiences sexual arousal psychologically. Samplings of her thoughts, feelings, and fantasies during intercourse were systematically compiled and classified. This was done by means of questionnaires and interview procedures which could be quantified and analysed statistically via computer programs. Care was taken to win the confidence of all those who participated in the studies, and there is good evidence that their responses were honest and open. Indeed, it turned out that the women were willing to reveal intimate data about certain areas of their sexual feelings that we, in our initial caution, thought should be avoided. As part of our studies, we also took samples of physiological responses from various areas of the body (for example, breasts, vagina, rectum, heart) under a number of different conditions.

The multiple sexual information obtained was in turn correlated with all that we could find out about each woman's personality. We examined traits, attitudes, and values – using techniques that probed at both conscious and unconscious levels. These techniques included well-standardized questionnaire measures of personality, projective tests like the Rorschach ink blots, word associations, and responses to special pictures designed to arouse emotional states. Furthermore, we used standardized methods for eliciting information about childhood experiences and patterns of relationships with one's parents. We wanted to find out whether – and if so how – a woman's sexual feelings are related to her entire personality and to her relationships with the important people in her life.

One of the major difficulties that arose in planning the studies of sexual responsiveness in women was to decide how such responsiveness could best be evaluated. Had it been feasible, it would perhaps have been ideal to observe subjects in the kind of setting devised by Masters and Johnson (*Human Sexual Response*, 1966) where overt behaviour during intercourse is recorded. However, this was not feasible; and one can argue rather persuasively (as have a number of critics of the Masters and Johnson work) that sexual behaviour and sexual attitudes are artificially distorted in a laboratory situation. For example, can a woman having intercourse on the 'scientific stage' feel tenderness or other shades of emotion towards her partner, feelings which might very well be of importance in more private, natural settings? Could one ask a woman having intercourse on the 'scientific stage' about her experiences and be able to differentiate those due to the strange bypassing of her privacy from those specific to sexual arousal? Of course, it would be foolish to assert that objective measures of individual variations in physiological response and other overt manifestations of emotion in a Masters-and-Johnson-type setting would not provide useful information about the psychological aspects of sexual arousal. But in my view such information would be supplemental rather than primary. Another possible approach to evaluating sexual responsiveness in women is to rely chiefly on 'quantity' measures like orgasm capacity and intercourse frequency, as has been customary in most studies (Kinsey, *et al.*, *Sexual Behavior in the Human Female*, 1953; Terman, *Psychological Factors in Marital Happiness*, 1938). However, such quantity measures obviously tell only a part of a complex story. Just as the gourmet could never adequately convey the nature of his gustatory experiences by recounting the amount he had eaten, a woman cannot communicate how sexual stimulation affects her by reciting the frequency with which she has an orgasm. This is not to say that the occurrence of orgasm is an unimportant aspect of sexual arousal, but it is only one aspect among many.

It would be well at this point to provide a detailed description of how we recruited the approximately three hundred women who participated in the studies and what was done to win their confidence. The first step in recruitment was to place an ad in the Syracuse University student newspaper which offered fifty dollars to married women (with at least a high-school education) in the 21–45 age range to participate in an experiment concerned with 'reproductive and menstrual functioning'. Participation was limited to married women in order to be certain that subjects would have had ample opportunity for sexual experience and also were currently engaging in regular intercourse. The requirement of a high-school education was introduced because many of the experimental procedures called for a fair degree of literacy and verbal fluency. An age restriction was imposed so as to control for possible physiological effects related to ageing.

It is important to note that the ad placed in the newspaper made no direct mention of the fact that the study was concerned with sexual behaviour. The women were explicitly told about the fact that they would be asked about their sexual behaviour only after they had telephoned for an appointment and actually come in for an interview to discuss the study. They were given the opportunity at that point to withdraw. About 10 per cent did withdraw. This general recruiting strategy was adopted in order to minimize biasing the samples with women who might, for their own reasons, be attracted to participating in a 'sex study'. As will be seen in data to be presented at a later point, a wide range of personalities was, indeed, obtained. For what it is worth, one may mention that the staff members in the laboratory who worked with the subjects were impressed with their diversity. There were the tense, the relaxed, the loud, the quiet, the shy, the exhibitionistic, the dull, the creative, the warm, the cold. A great many participated primarily for the rather substantial financial remuneration; some came for the adventure; some were secretly looking for help for family and sexual problems; some volunteered because a close friend who had decided to participate persuaded them to do so; and some were genuinely altruistic in their desire to help a scientific enterprise. My own impressions were that the two prime motivations were, first of all, financial and, secondly, the wish to do something novel and exciting.

It must be emphasized that although efforts were made to eliminate certain kinds of biased selectivity in the recruitment of the women, there was obviously no intent to obtain a sample representative of the average American woman. As will be shortly described, the women in the samples collected were more educated than average; their husbands were predominantly students (55 to 70 per cent) and eventually would attain high social status; they included only one black woman; and were largely Protestant in religious affiliation. It would, of course, have been ideal if truly representative samples could have been recruited; but to do so was beyond the resources of the laboratory in which the research was undertaken. The more modest goal was set of studying sexual responsiveness in women living in a small segment of the culture. No claims will be made concerning the availability of findings that emerged from this portion of society. Future work will decide whether our findings are applicable to society in general. However, it is reassuring that the frequencies of various patterns of sexual behaviour in the samples studied proved to be similar to those found by Kinsey, *et al.* (1953) in their middle-class samples.

A word should be said about the research strategy underlying the overall project. Seven separate samples of women were studied. This was done with the idea of checking and rechecking any positive findings that emerged. When a significant and meaningful result was obtained in one sample of women, it was not considered to be reliable until it could be duplicated in a number of subsequent samples. Several of the most important findings were reaffirmed in four separate instances in order to make sure of their solidity.

A considerable number of persons assisted in the collection of the research information. At various points there was participation by a gynaecologist, nurses, laboratory technicians, and an expert in the area of psychophysiological measurement. I particularly wish to highlight the role of my wife, Dr Rhoda Fisher, who is a clinical psychologist with special interests in the behaviour dynamics of women and the treatment of disturbed children. She took major responsibility for the intensive interviews which we conducted with many of the women. Her insights were invaluable in coming to grips with a number of difficult interpretative problems. Her emphatic and scientific understanding of women helped to broaden my horizons. Over the course of hundreds of hours of discussion her views permeated numerous of the formulations in this book.

The findings extracted from the studies were looked at to see how they either support or contradict previous reports in the literature dealing with sexual behaviour. When all of the facts were assembled, they strongly contradicted many widely accepted ideas about female sexuality. Obviously, they also raised doubts about certain important, widely used practical educational and treatment procedures which are derived from such false ideas. For example, it turned out that some of our formal modes of sex education are based on what are probably incorrect ideas about what facilitates sexual adjustment. There was also additional solid evidence that we have done injustice to many women by telling them that they need psychotherapeutic treatment for supposedly abnormal modes of sexual response – which are actually quite 'normal'. Let me repeat that the authority of the 'sex expert' has been considerable – both in professional and popular circles – and it may be that countless women have lived in a state of unhappiness as they have attempted to force themselves to conform to an ideal of sexual performance based on an erroneous theory of female sexuality.

The major purpose of this book is to review in a nontechnical way what is now actually known about sexual response and sexual experience in women. Hopefully this information will be of value not only because it concerns an important area of knowledge but also because it will enable people to make more rational decisions about their own sexual behaviour.

Part I. Research Findings

1. *Varieties of Normal Sexuality*

A survey of the scientific literature dealing with female sexuality reveals not only that women vary greatly with respect to their sexual behaviour but also with respect to the conditions they require for becoming sexually aroused. As shown by the reports of Kinsey, *et al.* (1953), Terman (1938, 1951), Chesser (1957), and others they differ radically in their frequency of intercourse, the kinds of foreplay they prefer, the range of sexual positions which appeal to them, the types of body stimulation which will excite them, and so forth. The average woman is relatively unaware of this diversity. She still knows very little about how other women experience the world of sexuality. She is acquainted with her own sexual feelings and experiences, but the chances are that she has rarely or ever heard another woman describe in detail her version of what sexual arousal is like. She lacks standards for judging how her own sexual reactions compare with the norm. This makes her feel uncertain about her own sexual behaviour and she may badly miscalculate her own sexual qualities

The actual range of normal female sexual preference is very great. There are married women who are satisfied with having sexual intercourse once or twice a week, but others are dissatisfied unless their intercourse rates are even ten times as great. Some women report that the essence of what they get out of intercourse is the orgasm experience. Others are much more rewarded by the body closeness and intimacy which intercourse provides. The ways in which women find it easiest and most enjoyable to reach orgasm with a male sex partner are amazingly diverse. One woman finds direct clitoral stimulation indispensable and another experiences such stimulation as painful – with all of her enjoyment derived from being vaginally penetrated. One seeks an extended period of foreplay involving massive sensory input into many areas of her body before penile stimulation produces orgasm. But another prefers a brief and sudden build-up of orgasmic excitement via penile intromission. Some women prefer sexual intercourse during the time of their menstrual flow; and others find that they are disgusted and inhibited by intercourse at this point in the menstrual cycle. They are most arousable just after the cessation of menstruation. It seems to be true that there are just as many effective modes for a woman to achieve enjoyable sexual arousal in her encounter with a man as there are ways for her to enjoy eating or to obtain zestful exercise of the large muscles of her body or to derive satisfaction from the aesthetic–artistic things in the world.

The process of a woman becoming sexually aroused is a highly individual matter. Each woman has her own unique pattern of experiences. I have discovered in the course of analysing such patterns that they can only be adequately conveyed from the inward, self-descriptive view of the individual woman. In one of our studies, which will be described later in greater detail, we asked a series of women to describe the manner in which each builds up to orgasmic excitement. They were given the following instructions:

Please give a detailed description of how you usually attain orgasm. Describe particularly the body sensations you experience, the thoughts that pass through your mind, your feelings, your attitudes, any difficulties you have, and so forth. Also describe in detail how you feel about five minutes *after* you attain orgasm.

Most of the women who participated in this study were able to write out rather full and meaningful descriptions of the arousal process and to convey well the inner subjective states accompanying it. A series of excerpts from their statements follows. They have been chosen so as to constitute a representative cross-section of the descriptions which were collected. They have been edited only to eliminate extraneous material and to guarantee the anonymity of the subjects. They vividly depict the varieties of the sexual experience in women.

Subject 1. To have the *most* enjoyable time in bed I prefer the setting to be romantic and pleasant. My husband is usually in an aggressive mood – which I prefer. I like to feel in a playful mood – and to talk and fool around for a while instead of getting right down to serious sex. I like a wide variety of foreplay including cunnilingus, fellatio, some anal stimulation occasionally. I like to feel as if my husband is paying strict attention to me and my pleasure – treating me in regal fashion. This is a selfish attitude – and, of course, I'm not treated like this *all* the time – but it is important to me to at least have this frame of mind. The physical actions can really fit the mental actions if you really believe this is the way things are. I like to feel relaxed and secure. I prefer to be held, petted, and in general treated gently. The orgasm itself builds from the foreplay. Often I have an orgasm during the foreplay – but prefer to have one during intercourse. Often I have orgasms – sometimes of lesser intensity – during foreplay and then experience another during intercourse. The sensation of the orgasm is one of mounting tension and warmth followed by a desire for more (whatever is happening at the moment), until finally a release and satisfaction is attained. When in a face-to-face position I prefer my husband to look at me – and this I find heightens the orgasm. It doesn't bother me too much if I don't attain orgasm – which isn't very often – because the sex was pleasurable anyway and I enjoy seeing my husband have fun. I do feel a little disappointed – but figure the next time will be better.

After lovemaking – I usually fall asleep – mainly because I'm tired. But if we do stay awake for a while the sensation is one of laziness, euphoria – sort of a floating, drifting, luxurious feeling. It is probably the happiest time of the day. I feel very secure, time seems suspended, and I feel as if I have no cares.

Subject 2. I almost always attain orgasm during intercourse – the majority of the time I have multiple orgasms. My husband and I change positions about three times on the average during intercourse (sometimes this doesn't mean a total change, just a shifting in one position, for example, I may lift my legs and wrap them around his waist after having them straight down when he's on top). This change in position stimulates different areas of our sex organs – fortunately, it works out that we both like the same angles of insertion at the same time. What happens many times is that I'll reach orgasm in one position and then we'll shift and I'll reach it again, etc., until my husband reaches a climax which in turn makes me climax again. The only times I don't reach climaxes like this are when my mind is on other things besides sex – if, for example, dinner is on the stove or I have a lot of things to do.

Sometimes I'll have climaxed a few times and be so tired I don't feel like continuing but I want my husband to climax and I'll force myself – then I'm usually happy about it and I reach orgasm again.

Orgasm for me usually involves getting more and more tense until there is a final release and then it drops down slowly. Actually I wish that release were more violent at times. Usually my orgasms are short periods – about fifteen seconds (although they have seemed much longer sometimes) of an intense, tingling, all-over feeling. Sometimes it would be nice if they were only about 5 seconds but more violent. Once this happened – when it was like a convulsive thing and I involuntarily and unconsciously screamed – and I really enjoyed it . . .

One thing about my orgasms – I feel like biting or grabbing something really hard and my husband's back sometimes gets pretty scratched.

Usually after orgasm, I feel like I have to urinate and almost always do go to the bathroom then. By the time I get out my husband is half asleep, and I soon fall asleep myself. If we ball during the day we usually fall asleep then too (we don't get as much sleep as we need), but often we get dressed and go out if it's the beginning of the day. At any rate, we both like to relax together for a little while afterwards.

Subject 3. My husband and I usually start out side by side. He does some foreplay around my face and breasts but usually moves on quickly to more intense stimulation. Often we are holding a conversation at this point at which I won't allow him to stimulate me in any part of the pelvic area since I'm not really concentrating on sex. The conversations tend to put me in a good mood, though, and when stopped leave me relaxed and more sensitive.

When my husband starts foreplay in the pelvic region I begin being more responsive. Before this time I'll play with his hair and stroke his body but until I am relaxed enough I don't like to touch his penis. The only words I can put or a reason is I have the feeling that it's 'ishy'. After I have started responding I no longer feel this way and enjoy stroking his penis.

Occasionally I feel if my husband would just move his hand slightly over, up or down, I would be stimulated better and quicker. Sometimes he does and I'm wrong, often I can't get him to the 'right' spot. Since I don't verbalize well at this time – still feeling embarrassed I think – this (my not opening my mouth and his inability to guess what to do) angers me and I end up impatient for the end. Also, I often take quite long to become stimulated. If I feel my husband is anxious, or think he is, or believe I am just taking too long, I also get angry at myself and impatient. Either way the result is of course to slow things down even more – once or twice to a standstill.

When my husband stimulates me in the clitoral region I usually get a tickling sensation. It is next to this area I want him to do most of his fingering. I usually find myself quite intently concentrating on what sensation I am feeling and how I would like him to move over his stimulation and where.

After the tickling sensation – as my husband stimulates me faster – I get a tingling in my legs which spreads up and kind of like hits my head. This is of course stronger at some times than at others – occasionally it is almost painful. Immediately after this happens the clitoral region is extremely sensitive and I don't want it touched.

It is only after I am through that I pull my husband over at which time we have intercourse. During this time I usually get great satisfaction from his enjoyment – since I've had mine. (I found if I waited for intercourse I did not reach orgasm, which left me very tense and irritable.) Rarely, I mentally wish he'd hurry up.

When we are finished I lie in the crook of his arm. I am very relaxed and in a good mood, feel very loving – not just sexually – toward my husband. I usually fall asleep quite quickly though occasionally I get the giggles and feel playful – but tired. I find that the next day I am also more cheerful and relaxed and friendly in general. (On the other hand, if I have not attained orgasm I lie wake for quite a while, irritated – physically and mentally – and awake the next morning still irritated – consequently I don't allow this to happen.)

Subject 4. We kiss deeply. I usually prefer undressing each other, but this depends on the circumstances. My husband fondles and kisses my breasts a great deal which I find quite exciting early in the experience (later, when I'm in a more excited state, my breasts do not add much). Sometimes, early in the experience, I must concentrate on what we are doing and consciously rid my mind of other thoughts in order to be really responsive. I am nearly always successful in doing this. I like to have my husband breathing into my ear as it helps me if I'm having trouble concentrating and it excites me simply physically and emotionally in that he is excited.

We spend most of the foreplay manipulating and/or kissing each other's sexual organs. This kissing is extremely exciting and I often reach orgasm once or twice at this time. The sensation is that of a rigid knot bursting and flowing suddenly; I feel very appreciative and in love. If this is the case, my husband will wait for my orgasm to subside and then re-excite me with his penis by rubbing the clitoris with shallow insertions. We then have intercourse during which I sometimes have what I suppose is a mild orgasm – and I become tense and excited again, though not to as great a degree as earlier and there is a fainter bursting release about the time of my husband's orgasm. If at this point, I do not experience another release, I nevertheless find it quite easy to relax after my husband's climax.

If I do not reach orgasm before intercourse, intercourse lasts longer with my husband withdrawing a number of times during it. This intensifies my excitement and prolongs my husband's and we generally reach a climax together. However, there have been times when one or the other of us has not reached orgasm this way (which practically never happens the other way).

This orgasm is deeper somehow. It takes a great deal more physical energy and is more emotionally satisfying in that I feel more at-oneness with my husband.

Five minutes after either of these types of orgasms, I feel very relaxed, at peace, cleansed. I feel very affectionate in a very deep and meaningful (as opposed to flirtatious) way. I nearly always fall asleep, if only for one-half hour. I very much dislike having to get out of bed immediately for any reason (my husband often gets up to turn off the light or whatever and gets back in bed peacefully – I find that very difficult to do – when I try, I feel uncomfortable – with the blood rushing to my head or even a suddenly hitting headache and/or a slightly nauseous, weak feeling). When I awake (if it's not during the night), I feel very replenished in a relaxed sort of way.

Subject 5. Before intercourse, during foreplay, which varies from one time to another, I go through a mental relaxation. My thoughts are on my body, my movements, my skin and my husband's. I concentrate on different things, such as the way our skin feels against each other and I concentrate on this for different areas of our bodies. It's as if I make every nerve in my body come alive and think.

Sometimes talking acts as a stimulus: talking about each other's bodies or sex organs, describing a certain feeling or even bringing up previous sexually satisfying experiences.

Usually we are both quite active, moving legs and arms over each other's bodies – even before any genital contact. When genital contact does happen – I am so 'psyched' for it that it's followed by a sigh. Then my thoughts are completely centred on how good his penis feels against my clitoris.

The way we approach intercourse depends a lot on our moods – if we are very quiet – i.e., if my love isn't expressed verbally but felt very deeply then we usually have much manual manipulation of the genitals or oral stimulation. If we are talkative and laughing before intercourse – we usually approach it more actively – using our entire body and body movements. At the time of genital contact with clitoral stimulation I begin to think about attaining an orgasm. It's as if all my feelings were condensed into one point. Sometimes I picture a plane with two dots – one is my brain and one my clitoris and there is an electric connection between the two.

Many times I try to picture what we look like and by doing so experience an exciting sensation.

With continued clitoral stimulation (and I am not only aware of my clitoris but his penis – I can concentrate on feeling one or the other). I finally seem to lose myself – or – until it is no longer only the clitoris that is excited but the entire area. Occasionally I picture in my mind what my genital area looks like. I finally have an ache deep in my vagina so profound that I have to have the penis inside. With its entrance – it's as if I had to hold my breath till it becomes completely inserted and then I relieve it with a very loud sigh or cry. It is at this point that my thoughts are of our union – no longer only of myself and my own feelings – I am very aware of my partner's feelings too. There is usually a brief period of just feeling the penis filling me – a lack of body movement. Soon our bodies move very deliberately and mechanically – it is then that my thoughts revert back to my own sensations – and I am working to increase the physical pleasure. My husband usually attains orgasm first which is followed by a pause, clutching each other, my need to hold him. However, the pause does not decrease my sensation – I have the mental satisfaction of knowing he is physically satisfied and I completely let go. It is rare that we attain orgasm at the same time, perhaps because I am too conscious of his nearness to it, I can't 'let myself go' knowing he is so close. However, once he has reached it – in no time I can also. As I again and completely concentrate on the feelings in my entire genital area. I reach a certain point when I know orgasm is inevitable and then almost hold it back to draw it out and cause a longer orgasm. I have absolutely no conscious thought of body movements or even of orgasm – I am only engrossed in the pleasurable sensation. The only images I have ever experienced at this time and during orgasm is a fuzzy blackness with red or white muted bursts coming through it. Orgasm comes with a dizziness, a loss of self – almost as if I didn't exist as a body but I exist on as a sensation. After orgasm my body completely relaxes – goes limp for a few seconds until I am conscious of what has really happened and how much my partner means to me. After intercourse we both lie close to each other quietly touching – talking some. I feel completely satisfied – almost relieved (as if there was a chance I might not attain orgasm). I feel very happy and full, close to another human being – amazed at the fact that there is such a pleasurable experience.

Subject 6. Attaining orgasm usually takes from five to fifteen minutes. I usually enjoy some love-making before intercourse actually starts. I enjoy breast stimulation, I find oral-genital relations extremely satisfying. If I am excited, I experience no pain during intercourse. Orgasm is attained only by clitoral stimulation.

I sometimes worry because it often takes me as much as fifteen minutes of stimulation before I can orgasm. The more I worry about how long it's taking, the longer it usually takes. I feel bad because, while my husband and I both agree that for me to orgasm is as important as for him, I feel that it must be tedious for him, and I have a hard time completely relaxing because I feel I am being selfish.

During orgasm I have no conscious thoughts, just a very pleasurable feeling of release.

After orgasm, I usually feel very satisfied, somewhat let-down, usually tired, but very comfortably tired. I usually like some love-making afterwards such as hugging, kissing, etc.

I often feel that during orgasm I have sort of left my husband for a few seconds and I like love-making after orgasm to re-establish the secure feeling of oneness.

Physical sensations after orgasm are heartbeat return to normal, breathing returns to normal. Vagina pulsates and throbs very strongly in a steady beat and then gradually stops. The general body feeling is a loss of energy and a general tiredness, but a feeling of satisfied tiredness.

Subject 7. Well, I like to play around a lot before, I like being romantic and my husband doesn't. He gets too excited and impatient. If we do play around a lot, he usually can't control himself. So, in that respect, I feel unsatisfied. We don't kiss and things for more than five minutes before he enters me. Before he does I usually like to play some more – but he gets his way. But then as soon as he does enter, I immediately feel extremely excited and become very passionate. It usually takes me quite a while to orgasm, but my husband can almost always stay with it. I usually feel a gradual build-up, but it is a very intense feeling of sexual excitement. We usually roll, twist, and turn and sometimes quickly get into a different position – usually without coming out. Then my husband can usually tell what's happening with me by the way I squeeze him or move. Or sometimes I even tell him. The thing that's usually on my mind is what I can do to make him feel better. When I do orgasm, it's always intense and nothing is running through my mind. Hardly ever don't my husband and I orgasm together. We squeeze tightly and finally relax. He stays in me for a few minutes and usually by this time I'm still not thinking – just feeling ecstatic. There are usually no difficulties.

Afterwards we separate and I feel completely relaxed and satisfied, calm and very womanly. I am usually conscious of not getting the bed messy now and usually feel the urge to urinate.

Subject 8. In attaining orgasm, some amount of foreplay is involved. It usually begins with kissing each other on the mouth, accompanied by each fondling the other. After about ten to fifteen minutes of foreplay, during which I have been clitorally stimulated and vaginally stimulated, my husband inserts his penis. My feelings up until this time have been a gradual mounting of tension (physical), my whole body tingles, and I am very highly excited. There is involved also breast stimulation. Generally, the body sensations while attaining orgasm are a tightening, physical tension, tingling.

The thoughts that pass through my mind are fleeting, mostly associated with my physical feeling.

There are some difficulties occasionally. Sometimes I'm worried that I won't have an orgasm, or that my husband won't be satisfied. These feelings do not last long, and seem to have no effect on attaining orgasm.

Five minutes after orgasm I am usually feeling good – satisfied, happy, and tired. There are times when I get depressed after orgasm – some kind of let-down. The depression doesn't last long.

Subject 9. We usually start out with long French kisses, while hugging each other tightly so that our bodies are pressed against each other. This generates a feeling of warmth and security between us. Then we engage in broad body caressing, which is the starting point of the actual stimulation. My husband fondles my breasts, often sucking on them. This doesn't arouse me greatly but brings on a feeling of satisfaction, as that of a mother breast-feeding a child. The breasts like this attention, making them become larger with erect nipples. He then stimulates my clitoris with his hand, often purposely avoiding it at first while just caressing the surrounding areas, so that I build up excitement in anticipation of the moment when he will actually touch the clitoris. When I feel nearly ready for orgasm, he inserts his penis in the vagina and begins intercourse. When he finally does insert his penis, it brings on a feeling of satisfaction that you're on the 'home stretch', after experiencing the anxieties and waiting for the overall stimulation of your body, so that you can easily receive the penis into the vagina. However, once he has entered me and started intercourse, I enter into another stage of anxiety waiting for the actual orgasmic climax. I often see myself climbing a mountain and finding it extremely steep at the top so that reaching the peak is more difficult than the climb thus far. My husband 'comes' shortly after entering my vagina, stops for a moment in his ecstasy, and then continues the humping movement until I reach orgasm. Just before this point I enter deep concentration on attaining my goal and at the exact moment that orgasm begins, I draw a complete blank of thoughts and just 'wallow' in the physical pleasure I derive. I sometimes have difficulty in attaining orgasm if I don't concentrate hard enough and find that my thoughts wander.

About five minutes after orgasm, I feel very peaceful and satisfied. I like to hug my husband tightly and hold him still inside me, symbolic of the feelings I have for our oneness and unity, and just lay in each other's arms, eking out every last ounce of satisfaction from the act. After all the waves of physical feeling and emotion have succumbed, I like to start over, omitting the foreplay and just repeating the actual motion of intercourse.

Subject 10. My vaginal secretions are only moderate; therefore quite a bit of stimulation is required to lubricate me enough for intercourse. My husband stimulates my clitoris and breasts until I attain orgasm – sometimes I masturbate while he stimulates my breast. I *always* have sexual fantasies while doing this – usually about how other men view me sexually. Afterward we rest very briefly – during which time I'm very tired, and feel intense affection for my husband. He then inserts his penis – there is usually some tightness, since orgasm has just been reached, but there is plentiful lubrication. But the tightness is alleviated with the body movements. My excitement mounts as his does, but my mind is more controlled; it's more of an intellectual excitement. I rarely fantasize at this point. I'm more aware of what *we* are doing as a unit and the gratification I'm giving him. The physical excitement that I experience at this time depends a lot on *pressure* – I feel the pressure of the penis and the more pressure the better. It only faintly resembles the same sensations as clitoral stimulation. The walls of the vagina feel practically nothing, the entrance feels more, the clitoris itself feels only a little tugging, a pleasant sensation, but not enough to induce a real climax. The most emotional sexual experiences occur when my husband enters me from behind – I feel a kind of subjugation to him – helplessness – the pressure is much greater as he goes much deeper – many times I reach an emotional peak – I feel ready to burst – and I end up crying hysterically for several minutes and recover after intercourse. It's a very happy and cathartic experience. But it's nevertheless a distinctly different experience from the pre-entry clitoral-stimulated orgasm. Afterwards, we're both very relaxed and fall asleep almost at once.

In general, one discerns in the various descriptions the well known sequence that proceeds from foreplay, through orgasm, to relaxation. First, there was foreplay, during which most of the women were touched and kissed on various body areas (for example, lips, breasts) and received manual and often oral stimulation of the clitoral region; next the women entered into active intercourse; and subsequently they reached orgasm either through the husband's penile intromission or his direct stimulation of some other body area (clitoris, breasts). Within this general pattern there were, however, great variations and a range of idiosyncrasies. One woman preferred not to begin the usual foreplay until her feet had been tickled for about ten minutes by her husband. Another enjoyed the sensation of air blown in her ear as part of the foreplay. Still another found that foreplay was greatly enhanced by having her husband blow air into her vagina. Some women attained orgasm one or more times during foreplay and others required an extended period to achieve even the minimal excitement needed to begin intercourse. During intercourse some used only one position and others changed positions several times before attaining orgasm. There were women who never reached orgasm but who said they found their general state of arousal satisfying. Interestingly, there were a few who never reached orgasm but who still responded to stimulation with great, almost overwhelming excitement. Some found that the experience of holding the penis in the vagina was necessary for orgasm, while others considered penile insertion as only detracting from their enjoyment. There were a few who considered it an important part of the arousal process to immerse themselves in elaborate make-believe sexual fantasies. Individual preferences for stimulation of a specific body part in attaining orgasm were often prominent. Illustratively, one woman found breast-sucking by her husband to consistently produce orgasm. For another woman rectal stimulation played such a role.

Each of the intercourse experience descriptions actually tells a different story with its own special dramatic quality and significance. Each woman perceives the events of intercourse within the context of her own unique problems and expectations. In summary, these are my impressions of what seem to be the most common themes.

1. Some women present intercourse primarily as a great adventure in which there are new experiences and sensations to be sampled. Emphasis is placed upon the range of positions used, the novelty of some of the sensations aroused, and the potential for unlimited exploration by each spouse of the other spouse's body.

2. Related to this first theme is the perception of intercourse as a means of attaining ecstasy or going on a 'trip' in which there are strange sensations and loss of identity. Included in this category are those who wish to ascribe a religious or mystical quality to sexual arousal.

3. For some women intercourse is an opportunity to prove their superior prowess in an activity that is highly valued. They dwell on their responsiveness, their ability to attain multiple orgasms, and the fact that they exceed their husbands in sexual capacity.

4. Another theme found in the intercourse descriptions portrays intercourse primarily as an opportunity for intimacy and blending oneself with a sex partner. Much is said about closeness, skin contact, cuddling, and feeling unbelievably united to another

human being. The process of joining with someone is depicted as comforting and anxiety-allaying.

5. A troubled martyred stance appears in some. The women in this category see intercourse as either painful or unpleasant. They picture themselves as victims of an inability to respond adequately to sexual stimulation. They dwell on their irritability during intercourse and their anticipation of ultimate frustration.

6. One interesting group characterizes sexual excitement as almost too intense to tolerate. They refer to their state of sexual arousal as painfully intense and suggest that they can barely control the tension that builds up. Illustratively, one woman said that when she became highly aroused sexually she was 'ready to climb the walls'. Reference is also made to excited body areas feeling 'sore' and oversensitive. Sexual excitement seems to be regarded as a force greater than oneself, with potential overwhelming and disorganizing properties.

7. There are also those who adopt a no-nonsense, 'business-like' attitude. They describe intercourse as a routine, well-practised procedure which provides adequate gratification, but which is simply one of a number of other important life activities. Several of the women who conveyed this idea indicated that shortly after intercourse they often resume some household task or work which needs to be done.

8. Finally we should mention those who experience intercourse as a reaffirmation of female identity. They speak of how 'womanly' they feel during and after sexual arousal. They experience sexual arousal as a demonstration that a man has accepted them in the role of 'real' woman.

This brief review of the patterns discerned in the intercourse descriptions is not in any sense offered as a definitive schema. It merely reflects an impressionistic analysis.

As already suggested in the descriptions presented above, the marked differences in the ways women experience sexual excitement extend into the domain of the orgasm. The next chapter will consider the extreme individual variations which exist with regard not only to what it takes to attain orgasm – but also with respect to whether orgasm occurs at all.

2. *The Female Orgasm: Myths and Facts*

It has recurrently puzzled those who have tried to understand female sexuality that so many women have difficulty in attaining orgasm. As a group, women seem to have more problems in building up to orgasmic excitement than do men. Numerous investigators (for example, Terman, 1951; Kinsey, *et al.*, 1953) have found that, in samples of married women, about 30 per cent either never achieve orgasm or do so only occasionally. One can also find more extreme reports (for example, Kinsey, *et al.*, 1953) which suggest that as many as 50 per cent of married women do not reach orgasm more than occasionally. It must be added at this point that there should be no simple equation of orgasm with sexual responsiveness. As will become clear further on, sexual responsiveness and orgasm capacity need to be considered quite separately. There are many women who never attain orgasm but who nevertheless enjoy intercourse and the sensations aroused by various forms of sexual stimulation (Chesser, 1957). However, orgasm still remains an important aspect of sexual arousal. Most women seek the release and gratification of orgasm. Although sexual satisfaction and orgasm are not synonomous, the experience of orgasm must remain one of the central concepts in any discussion of sexual behaviour.

The fact that women have more orgasm difficulties than men is especially puzzling in the light of evidence mustered by Masters and Johnson (1966) that the physiological processes involved in the female orgasm are analogous to those in the male orgasm. The puzzle becomes even more confusing when one considers that Masters and Johnson and others have found that the average woman is more capable than the average man of experiencing multiple orgasms within a limited time span. One psychoanalyst, Sherfey (1966), who has examined in minute detail male-female orgasm patterns, considers the female orgasm potential to exceed the male's tremendously.

As I became acquainted with the accumulated scientific facts relating to female sexuality, it was this problem of women often having to struggle to reach orgasm which was the most mystifying. I became intrigued with its implications and decided to extract from the literature all the major explanations that had been offered and also the scientific evidence bearing upon their validity. I found that many different perspectives had been taken. Let us examine them.

Mental Health

A favourite theory, particularly popular in psychoanalytic circles, is that the woman who cannot reach orgasm is a psychologically flawed person. Presumably, her orgasm difficulty is merely a reflection of her overall maladaptive character structure. She is seen as one who is significantly disturbed and lacking in ego integration. It is said that she is struggling with unconscious conflicts which make her anxious and unstable; and her orgasm inhibition is only one facet of her total disequilibrium. Many kinds of deep unconscious conflicts have been presumed to be linked to the orgasm problem. One finds in the psychoanalytic literature that they are often attributed in one way or another to the classic Oedipal dilemma. But they have also been variously and esoterically depicted as relating to 'penis envy', 'fears of body dissolution', and guilt-laden 'oral sadistic' fantasies. It is no exaggeration to state that one can find almost an infinite number of 'basic conflicts' cited in the psychiatric literature to explain what is considered to be the flawed ego structure of the woman with orgasm difficulties. The basic premise of this orientation is that an orgasm problem is merely a 'symptom' of a more general kind of disability. To have orgasm problems is an indication that a woman is seriously neurotic or even worse. The very definition of a 'satisfactory' orgasm is quite strict in psychoanalytic circles. It is assumed that only an orgasm produced by the movement of the penis in the vagina is a mature form of sexual fulfilment. Orgasm produced by manual or oral stimulation of the clitoris is labelled 'immature'. A woman who does not achieve consistent 'vaginal orgasm' is regarded as maladjusted. This view has been widely defended despite the fact that Kinsey, *et al.* (1953) and Masters and Johnson (1966) have presented evidence suggesting that the so-called vaginal orgasm is based on indirect stimulation of the clitoral area.

What does the empirically and experimentally derived scientific literature have to say about the relationship between orgasm capacity in women and their psychological health? In general, it tells us that this relationship has been grossly exaggerated. Mental health and orgasm capacity simply cannot be equated. If one consults all of the existing pertinent studies, one finds that the majority of them cannot detect correlations between orgasm consistency and measures of psychological stability or soundness. There are a few scattered studies in which small correlations have been found; but they are wholly overshadowed by the majority, in which little correlation is found. One report described a sample of schizophrenic women as *more* sexually responsive than a sample of neurotics (Coppen, 1955), and in several studies schizophrenic women were found to be just as orgasmic as normal women (for example, Winokur, Guze, and Pfeiffer, 1959). In another study involving unmarried college girls, it was observed that the girls who were most orgasmic showed the *least* personality stability. Perhaps, surprisingly, we are even told by one investigator (Pomeroy, 1965) that prostitutes successfully experience orgasm in their personal, 'non-commercial' intercourse more frequently than normal women do. He notes too that over 20 per cent of the prostitutes experience orgasm often while having intercourse with their customers. It is generally agreed that most women who become prostitutes are seriously maladjusted, immature, and depreciatory in their attitude toward themselves. But despite this apparent maladaptive role, prostitutes turn out to be relatively highly orgasmic.

In the face of the scientific evidence it is no longer justifiable to assert that a woman who has difficulties in reaching orgasm is clearly psychologically disturbed. The burden of proof now rests upon those who insist upon maintaining such a view. As I will suggest later, it is time that we stop classifying women in terms of one aspect of their behaviour.

Sex Partner and Practice Effects

Another favourite explanation of female orgasm inhibition revolves around the ineptitude of the male sex partner. In this view every woman has a reasonable potential for orgasmic arousal if only her sex partner is sufficiently wise and adept to stimulate her properly. The stereotype of the potent male figure, as it has been promulgated in the popular culture and by novelists (for example, Norman Mailer), presents such a man as one whose prowess extends to being able to stimulate orgasm in women to a degree that other men cannot match. From this viewpoint a woman who cannot reach orgasm need only find a more expert sex partner; or – another possibility – her inept sex partner can be trained to do a better job. The wave of sex manuals that has cascaded over the contemporary scene arises at least partially from this orientation. The writers of sex manuals offer to teach artful, clever, and gymnastic strategies which will inexorably drive a woman to orgasmic intensity. A woman's capacity for orgasm is represented as being primarily a function of the skill that her sex partner can bring to bear upon her. The natural conclusion of this view is that if a woman does not attain orgasm, the fault lies in the deficiencies of her sex partner. Multitudes of men whose wives cannot build up to orgasmic arousal have laboured under this stigma and struggled with a sense of guilt. Perhaps even more poignantly, they have, in their self-blame, belittled their own masculinity and therefore marred a central aspect of their identity. (Incidentally, some of the leaders in the Women's Lib movement have been especially attracted to the 'deficient sex partner' explanation because it fits well with their accusatory stance towards men.)

One of the ideas implicit in the concept that an 'expert' can produce orgasm where others cannot is that the process of building up sexual excitement is a skill, almost like that involved in athletic attainment, which can be improved by practice. The sex manuals are explicit in giving this message. It is suggested that if a woman will practise sex in certain ways she will improve her arousal capabilities. The promise is made that practice will give those unable to reach orgasm the skills ultimately to do so. Learning to build up to orgasmic excitement is regarded as quite analogous to mastering any complicated motor task.

What is actually known about the importance of a woman's sex partner in helping her to reach orgasm? Aside from delivering a certain minimum necessary amount of stimulation, does he have the potentiality of greatly increasing or decreasing a woman's likelihood of building up orgasmic excitement? Kinsey and his associates concluded from their findings that the sexual techniques employed by the male do not have much influence on a woman's sexual responsiveness. Several others have reported that a woman's sexual responsiveness is not correlated with how long her husband stimulates her before or during intercourse. They have also noted that her responsiveness is not related to how sexually experienced her husband was before their marriage or how potent he has been subsequently.

Efforts have been made to see if the husbands of high- and low-orgasmic women differ. Questions have been asked as to whether they were brought up in unlike ways or have different character traits? Terman (1938, 1951) carried out two thorough studies in which he appraised husbands of women whose degree of sexual responsiveness was known. He looked at every conceivable aspect of these men. For example, he evaluated their religious background, early sex instruction, attitudes toward parents, shyness, childhood happiness, and so forth. He concluded that there were no reliable links between the husband's qualities and the sexual responsiveness of the wife. The husband of the highly orgasmic woman was not detectably unlike the husband of the low orgasmic woman. Such findings suggest that the qualities of the sex partner may not be as important in determining a woman's arousal as many have thought. Of course, we still have a great deal more to learn about this matter. It can only be said that at this point the evidence is rather negative. This is especially true with regard to the importance of differences in the kinds of sex techniques husbands use and also the durations of stimulation they apply. The woman who is having trouble achieving orgasm in her contacts with a man who conscientiously tries to stimulate her and who decides that what she needs is a sex partner with 'better technique' is probably not correct in her assumption. However, the door should not be closed on the possibility that a man with one type of personality as compared to another may be better able to elicit orgasm from a particular woman. We have to wait and see what future research reveals about this issue.

One other point should be mentioned. It is pretty solidly known that the greater a woman's orgasmic capacity the more she considers her marriage to be a happy one. Does this mean that a husband with whom a woman can live happily is able to excite her more sexually? It is not easy to separate what is cause and what is effect. Perhaps a woman who is reaching orgasm consistently in her marital coitus does for this reason alone experience her marriage as happier than the woman who is failing to reach orgasm. In other words, it can just as easily be said that a happy relationship with one's spouse increases a woman's orgasm ability as it can be said that orgasm success increases satisfaction with the marriage. Discussion of this matter gets further complicated when we learn that in some studies there is no correlation between the wife's orgasmic ability and how happy her husband considers the marriage to be. This would imply that his feelings about the marriage do not materially influence his ability to excite his wife sexually. This brings to mind the fact that a group of alcoholic men, who would be expected to be very unhappy, were found in one study (Burton and Kaplan, 1968) to be just as capable of producing orgasm in their wives as normal, non-alcoholic men. Also, there are conflicting reports about whether women and men who are at the point of divorce are less able to arouse each other sexually than spouses in stable marriages. One would doubt that a woman's marital happiness and her orgasm capacity will finally turn out to be related in any *simple* way.

As mentioned, many so-called sex manuals preach that a woman can increase her sexual responsiveness by perfecting her sexual skills. Presumably, she can cultivate her orgasmic capacities in the same way that an athlete can become more proficient by diligent practice; her ability to reach orgasm is put in the same category as learning to play golf or ski. Many have learned that there is limited validity in this view. There are millions of women who have practised sex intensively for years and been completely unable to attain orgasmic excitement. This is not to suggest that practice has zero effect upon sexual responsiveness, but rather that the effect is not a large one.

The scientific findings about the role of practice are complex and perhaps confusing. There are observations which, at first sight, support the idea that orgasmic response is affected by experience. First, Schofield (1965) found that only 28 per cent of a sample of teen-aged girls reached orgasm at the time of their first intercourse. This is somewhat lower than the proportion (49 per cent) of women who reach orgasm after only one month of marriage (as reported by Kinsey and his associates). This difference could be interpreted as due to the impact of a month of sexual practice, although other explanations (for example, increased physiological maturity, decreased tension associated with the legalization of intercourse for the married) could be offered. Second, we find that in the original Kinsey studies 75 per cent of married women reported they attained at least occasional orgasm during the first year of marriage; 83 per cent by the fifth year; and 89 per cent by the twentieth year. It was also found that whereas only 49 per cent of women had reached orgasm in the first month of marriage, 55 per cent had in the second month, and 59 per cent by the third month. In a three-month span there was a 10 per cent increase. Relatedly, 39 per cent of females were reaching orgasm in all or nearly all of their coitus during the first year of marriage and by the end of the twentieth year of marriage this percentage had increased to 47 per cent. Such increasing proportions of successful orgasm sound like they could be based on practice.

But what about the size and significance of these practice effects? Let us focus more closely on some of the findings that were cited. When we do so we find that from the first to the fifth year of marriage there was a reported 8 per cent decrease in women who could not attain orgasm at all. There was a 3 per cent decrease from the fifth to the tenth year of marriage; a 2 per cent decrease from the tenth to fifteenth year; and a 1 per cent decrease from the fifteenth to the twentieth year. Over the entire span (from first to twentieth year of marriage) there was a 14 per cent decrease in women who could not attain orgasm at all. This is really not very impressive. After the first five years of intensive marital coitus only 8 per cent of the women who could not attain orgasm at all managed to learn to achieve orgasm 'occasionally'! In the next five years of intensive practice only another 3 per cent learned how to have an occasional orgasm. It is also disappointing to learn that after twenty long years of experience only 8 per cent more women were able to master the problems of attaining orgasm at a level of high consistency. Thousands of intercourse experiences resulted in relatively little improvement in this category. Generally, then, it would be fair to say that sexual practice can increase orgasm capacity, but that the return is limited. It would probably be a rare instance in which a woman who could not reach orgasm in her early intercourse contacts was transformed into a person of high orgasm consistency because she had the opportunity for repeated sexual experiences. This is an important fact to communicate to those who look to learning new techniques from sex manuals as a way of rescuing themselves from sexual response difficulties. It will save a good deal of disappointment.

Social Class and Education

There are those who imagine that the unspoiled primitive woman has no difficulty in achieving orgasm. They think that the simple woman, close to nature, is effortlessly consumed by orgasmic passion, and that the Western woman's orgasm dilemmas derive from the artificiality of her life. The Western woman is viewed as too separated from her natural heritage by education and the props of possessing money and material possessions. She is regarded as one whose natural femininity has been driven out of her by the masculine-tinged educational procedures of our culture. It is assumed that becoming well-educated encases a woman in a veneer of masculine values which prevent her from responding with feminine spontaneity to sexual stimulation. Also, when a woman acquires the highly 'civilized' foibles and fashions that define being a woman of social status, she is thought to be shutting herself off from her natural functioning self, which responds to sexual arousal with unencumbered directness. The orgasmic woman is thought of as the stereotype of the 'native maiden' in a tribal culture or the 'peasant woman' living and working in intimate touch with the earth. She is even presumed to be better typified by the lower-class poor girl than the upper-class rich girl.

Again, the facts do not support this expectation. Numerous studies (for example, Kinsey, *et al.*, 1953) have shown that the higher a woman's socio-economic status, the more consistently she achieves orgasm. It is the upper- rather than the lower-class woman who gets most sexually aroused. This is affirmed by several investigators (for example, Rainwater, 1965) who intensively interviewed lower-class Mexican, Puerto Rican, American, and English married women. They discovered that these women did not, in general, enjoy sexual intercourse. For them, it was more a wifely duty than a source of gratification. One explanation offered for the lower-class woman's sex inhibitions is based on the nature of her relationship with her husband. It is pointed out that the husband's and the wife's roles in the lower classes are highly differentiated and there is little mutuality or motivation for intimate exchange. The division of labour within the family is carefully and rigidly spelled out. This contrasts sharply with the middle-class family in which husband–wife roles are less precisely differentiated and there is a greater emphasis on close communication between spouses. The psychological separation between lower-class husband and wife which is linked to their strict roles in life may make it difficult for them to exchange love and tenderness; and so the wife, especially, may find intercourse a mechanical arrangement which is too impersonal to turn her on. By way of contrast it is noted that in the middle-class relationship (Rainwater, 1965, p. 77):

> The emphasis on sharing in such relationships extends to sex so that it becomes important that the wife also find enjoyment in sex-

uality; and that the husband not be 'selfish' by taking pleasure only for himself. The husband must help his wife to achieve gratification, and the wife must achieve it to prove to herself that she is really participating as she should and to provide her husband with the fuller gratification that is believed to come when the wife achieves orgasm also.

The so-called frigid woman is at times popularly associated with the figure of someone who is very intellectual and who has had too much education for her own good. It is widely believed that education saps a woman of her femininity and her ability to be passionate; but a survey of the empirical facts provides quite a different viewpoint. Kinsey, *et al.* (1953) found that among married women orgasm capacity is higher at the upper as compared to the lower levels of education. Kinsey, *et al.* state (p. 378):

> In every period of marriage, from the first until at least the fifteenth year, a larger number of the females in the sample who had more limited educational backgrounds had completely failed to respond to orgasm in their marital coitus, and a smaller number of the better educated females had so completely failed.

Incidentally, such orgasm differences were observed despite the fact that there were no differences in intercourse frequency among educational levels.

Religion and Puritanical Values

A particularly popular concept of what is wrong with the non-orgasmic woman is that she is constrained by the antisex values which she has learned from the religious forces in her life. It is pointed out that most of the major religious systems regard sexual activity with suspicion and give the message that sexuality is probably evil. Puritanical views of sex obviously abound and there is no question that the growing girl is often inculcated with negative and guilty feelings about her own sexual sensations. Masters and Johnson (1966) have, on the basis of their clinical experience, attached considerable importance to the role of religiously derived inhibitions in interfering with sexual responsiveness, both in women and men. The nun who has taken the vow of chastity provides the core image of how religious constraints can apparently deprive a woman of her sexual being. The psychiatric literature too contains profuse examples of cases in which women are said not to be able to respond sexually because of the severity of their early religious training.

Overlapping with this emphasis on the negative effect of religion is the position that poor 'sex education' cripples many women sexually. There is a widely prevalent sentiment that when a woman is reared in a context where sex is a secretive matter and she cannot acquire realistic facts about reproduction and the nature of the sex act, she cannot become a sexually responsive person. It is considered that her years of 'ignorance' concerning important sexual facts leave her grossly 'scarred' and likely to be shocked or overwhelmed by the true nature of sex with a man when she finally experiences it. A deficient 'sex education' is depicted as harmful, not only because it suggests a negative attitude towards sex on the part of the parents who have neglected their obligations in this area, but also because it deprives a girl of fundamental facts which she needs to construct a realistic and mature concept of sexuality.

Quite a number of studies have been undertaken to explore the relationship between orgasmic capacity and religious orientation. Kinsey, *et al.* (1953) included questions about religiosity and religious membership in their survey of sexual behaviour. While they discovered that religiosity plays a role in how sexually active women are premaritally, it proved to be of little significance for married women. In the setting of legitimatized marriage, they could find no relationship between a woman's ability to attain orgasm and her religious devoutness. They could also find no clear orgasm differences among Protestant, Catholic, and Jewish women. Further, there were no correlations between religiosity and the frequency of intercourse. The great majority of other investigations in this area have come up with essentially the same results.

It is true that a few reports do suggest the possibility that extremely drastic disapproval of sex by a religious sect may have negative effects upon the sexual responsiveness of women who are reared within that sect. One observer (Goshen-Gottstein, 1966) has described an ultra-orthodox Jewish group living in Israel in which the severity of disapproval of sexual behaviour is paralleled by the fact that married women seem rarely or never to attain orgasm. It should be added that Kinsey and his associates also noted a trend for very highly devout Catholic women to have more difficulty reaching orgasm during the first year of marriage than 'inactive' Catholics and Protestants and Jews in general. But the actual size of the difference was really quite small. The devout Catholic woman was not dramatically less orgasmic than the non-devout Protestant woman – but simply several percentage points lower.

Although there is no question that religious teachings about sex have great influence on sexual conduct, it is doubtful whether they have a general inhibiting impact on the ability of a woman to build up orgasmic excitement when she is having intercourse with her husband. Those who wish to place the burden upon organized religion for sexual inadequacy in women cannot find much support for their position in the available evidence.

The view that religious forces have negative effects on sexual responsiveness is expressed in the related idea that a puritanical or secretive attitude toward sexual matters has a similar negative impact. Neglect in providing proper 'sex education' is often singled out as a prime example of how parents' overmoralistic or repressive attitudes toward sex may result in their handicapping their offspring in making an adequate sexual adjustment. The reluctance of the parents to provide realistic notions about the nature of sexual intercourse is portrayed as giving their offspring a negative, inhibited, and fearful concept of sexuality. This is a widely accepted view and somehow appealing in its logic. But the facts in the scientific literature do not fit the expected mould. Two extensive studies by Terman (1938, 1951) in which women were questioned about their early sex education and also their ability to attain orgasm, revealed a complete absence of relationship between these two variables. Orgasm capacity was not correlated with how adequate sex education had been or with the source or sources from which a woman had learned the primary 'sex facts'.

Physical, Hormonal, and Age Factors

A strictly biological theory of sexual responsiveness seeks explanations in terms of hormone levels, attributes of the body, and maturational phenomena. If a woman fails to achieve orgasm, according to this theory, it is because of a deficiency in some biological structure or function. It is probably true that, over the years, many women with orgasm difficulties have been 'treated' with hormonal or other chemical substances. A woman's sexual inhibition may be attributed to the fact that she is too masculine in her body build or lacks a proper amount of a specific sex-linked hormone. There have been studies which have tried to demonstrate that a woman's sexual responsiveness is dependent upon the immediate phase of the menstrual cycle in which she receives sexual stimulation. Each phase may then be defined in terms of hormonal shifts. A young, unfeminine-appearing woman who cannot build up to orgasmic excitement may be 'diagnosed' as delayed in her sexual maturity. This is particularly likely if she has a history of a chronologically late onset of menstruation or various secondary sex characteristics. Even the presence of symptoms like painful or irregular menstrual periods may encourage such a view. If a woman develops sexual response problems in her later years, they may be attributed to the ageing process; they may be specifically blamed on the physiological alterations linked with menopause. Some have also attempted to trace response difficulties to the fact that a woman has not experienced pregnancy which is thought to produce changes in body structures which favour orgasmic build-up. The biological model of feminine sexual arousal would minimize the significance of social and psychological factors.

Incidentally, an emphasis upon the role of the biological in sexual responsiveness carries with it the notion that ageing will drastically reduce capacity. Presumably, as a woman's body grows older, it loses its vigour or vitality and the response to sexual stimulation falls off. The ability to reach orgasm is viewed as a manifestation of a vigorous body and is thought to decline as the body declines.

In fact, intense response to sexual stimulation is not the monopoly of the young female. Within a wide range, older married women are just as able to reach orgasm as younger ones. Kinsey, *et al.* (1953), Masters and Johnson (1966), and others have almost unanimously declared that a woman can retain her sexual responsiveness into the sixties and seventies. Kinsey suggested that some of the apparent decline in intercourse frequency and responsiveness attributed to ageing married women may be due to the more obvious physiological decline of their husbands. One source (Pfeiffer, *et al.*, 1968) found that some women even show increased sexual interest when they reach advanced ageing.

It is pertinent to the matter of age that Kinsey, *et al.* found that married women born after 1900 displayed greater orgasm consistency than women born before 1900. Also, married women born in each of the three decades following 1900 showed a marked trend to attain greater orgasm consistency than women born in each of the decades preceeding it. The increase in orgasm consistency over the sequence of decades represents a good example of how cultural conditions may affect sexual responsiveness in women. That is, one may presume that the increase reflects the effects of changing social conditions during this time period. As will be specified later, the crucial component of these changing conditions probably relates to new attitudes that parents have adopted toward the individuality and strength of their daughters.

The fact that women retain their orgasmic capacity well into old age is one of a number of lines of evidence suggesting that hormonal factors are relatively unimportant in a woman's responsiveness. Large hormonal changes occur in the post-menopausal woman but they do not lead to changes in orgasm consistency. Similarly, gross hormone changes related to the pregnancy cycle do not seem to affect sexual response. Various studies have failed to find relationships between orgasm capacity and such factors as age of onset of menstruation and other indicators of puberty, breast size, and measures of physique. It should be added that women who have been pregnant one or more times are no more sexually responsive than women who have never had a child. This contradicts long-existing folk beliefs that a 'frigid' woman can somehow be 'cured' by going through the pregnancy experience. At this point it is fair to say that there is no proof that the female orgasm is regulated by specific hormones. There is also no evidence that any one particular kind of female body configuration is superior to others in its orgasm potential.

Traumatic Episodes

Both in the psychiatric literature and in popular lore one finds the assumption that a woman's ability to be sexually responsive may be 'ruined' by a dramatic sexual trauma. It is exemplified in the image of the woman who is frightened by sex and unable to become aroused by a man because anything sexual conjures up anxiety-laden memories of a previous rape or 'attack' experience. The sex trauma which may be blamed for a woman's inhibitions may be variously linked to witnessing intercourse between her parents, being 'caught' in the act of masturbating, or serving as the victim of a sadistic sex act. Sexual difficulties are, from this perspective, the aftermaths of events, usually occurring fairly early in life, which had dramatically shocking impact. It is often a derivative assumption that if the sexually inhibited woman can be made clearly aware of the source of her disturbance and is given the opportunity to gain insight into how she has irrationally tied all sexuality to one traumatic episode, she can regain the ability to become fully passionate.

If one looks at scientific reports, rather than novels about heroines who cannot enjoy sex because of a past sex trauma, one finds that the impact of dramatic episodes has been exaggerated. Many of the studies which have investigated sexual responsiveness in women – for example, Terman, 1938, 1951 have inquired about previous traumatic sexual experiences. They have all largely failed to detect a convincing link between orgasm capacity (or any other measure of sexual responsiveness) and reports of previous sexual experiences which were disturbing either because they were frightening or inept in character. One observer (Shope, 1966) actually reported that unmarried girls who were able to reach orgasm had had *more* shocking sexual encounters before the age of sixteen than girls unable to attain orgasm. Another source (Kanin and Howard, 1958) which focused on honeymoon behaviour could find few instances in which long-term marital-sex adjustment was disturbed by the negative or disappointing quality of honeymoon interactions. One of the most convincing bits of evidence concerning this general issue came out of a study which looked at the sexual responsiveness of women in their marital relations who had experienced abortion prior to the marriage (Gebhard, Pomeroy, Martin, and Christenson, 1958). The abortions were largely illegal, and there is little doubt that they were highly disturbing. One might think that they would leave an indelible negative imprint upon a woman's sexual perspective. However, there was no evidence that the woman who had had an abortion was any less orgasmic after her marriage than the woman who had not been subjected to an abortion. It is, of course, conceivable that in a small number of extreme cases a woman's sexual adaptation could be drastically shaped by one terrifying incident. But overall, it looks as if the import of such incidents has been falsely magnified. As will be discussed later, a woman's orgasm capacity seems to evolve out of a complex, long-term series of conditions, rather than being determined by what happens in one incident in her life.

Comment

My review of what is actually scientifically known about orgasm capacity turned out to be largely negative in its findings. Quite a number of favourite stereotyped notions about sexual responsiveness in women are simply not justified by the facts. The religious woman is no less responsive than the one without religious ties. The well-educated female is more, rather than less orgasmic than the poorly educated one. It is not true that education renders women less sensitive to sexual stimulation. Similarly, the woman of low social class is not more, but rather less orgasmic than the woman of higher social class. The concept of the lower-class woman as being 'earthy' and 'natural' and therefore especially sensuous does not hold up. One of the most surprising things that has emerged is that intensive practice of intercourse seems to have a small effect on orgasm capacity. Only a small percentage of women who have orgasm difficulties learn to achieve orgasm consistently even after twenty years of marital coitus. The major 'improvement' produced by years of marital intercourse is that it enables a sizeable percentage of women who could not reach orgasm at all to do so 'occasionally'. Most of the 'improvement' occurs in the first five years of marriage and tapers off to just a few percentage points in succeeding five-year blocks, up to twenty years. The smallness of 'practice effects' raises serious doubts about how much a woman can hope to increase her orgasm potential by consulting 'sex manuals' and trying out new gymnastic intercourse techniques. Just as surprising as the scientific facts about 'practice' were those having to do with the qualities of the sex partner. Contrary to the belief of many women that they would become highly orgasmic if they could only just find the 'right man', no one has been able to show a correlation between orgasm capacity and the attributes of the sex partner. The woman whose husband has had much sex experience prior to marriage is no more likely to reach orgasm than one whose husband has had little experience. There is no indication that husbands of orgasmic women have different personalities than husbands of the nonorgasmic. While there still remains a good deal more scientific work to be done in order to finally validate these conclusions, the fact remains that at this time the burden of proof falls on those who place partial or full responsibility on the sex partner for a woman's orgasm difficulties. Finally, it is important to call attention to the fact that no one has been able to demonstrate that the female orgasm is tied to hormonal or physique factors. There does not seem to be a particular type of female body which is more sexually arousable than other types.

The analysis of the existing stock of facts about female sexuality which has just been presented left me with a sense of disappointment and confusion. Not a single one of the current and often widely accepted theories concerning the determinants of a woman's orgasm capacity seemed to be even slightly supported by what is scientifically known. These theories suddenly looked very insubstantial. I would like to emphasize that it was not our intent to prove or disprove any specific theory or to find support for any pet notions of our own. Our aim was simply to find out what was dependably true.

The remainder of this book will be devoted to a series of studies which were instituted in my laboratory as a beginning of an attempt to fill the scientific vacuum which seemed to exist with respect to the nature of female sexuality.

3. Studies of Orgasm Behaviour

It was against the background of negative and disappointing facts just described that my colleagues and I set out to learn more about the conditions which govern sexual responsiveness in women. As I noted in the Preface, the women who volunteered for our seven research study groups were largely in their early or middle twenties. They averaged about two or three years of college education, and typically had one child or less. About 35 – 45 per cent were Protestant; 20 – 30 per cent, Catholic; and about 15 per cent Jewish. Only one black and no Orientals were represented. Obviously, the women studied were a select group; and it remains to be seen whether the results which were obtained can be applied to women in general. However, I privately believe that the women studied will prove to be representative of the middle-class Western woman.

Great effort was put into winning the confidence of the women who participated. This seemed essential in order to obtain accurate information about their sexual behaviour. No sexual questions were asked of them until they had a good chance to get to know the personnel conducting the study – and to trust them. Many aspects of their sexual behaviour and feelings were explored with them, by means of both questionnaires and interviews. Each woman was particularly asked to describe the nature of her orgasm experiences. She not only wrote a description of how she and her husband stimulated each other while having intercourse, but also indicated how consistently she attained orgasm. She rated the nuances of feeling and sensations she experienced during and after orgasm. She was asked for information about foreplay, preferred intercourse positions, strength of orgasm, multiple orgasms, and the areas of her body that are most and least arousable. She was also requested to provide information about the following:

Timing of own orgasm as compared to husband's
Feelings during first intercourse experience
Intercourse frequency
Preferred intercourse frequency
Conditions most preferred for intercourse
Preferences for clitoral versus vaginal stimulation
Vaginal sensations
Breast sensations
Muscular control during sexual excitement
Vaginal secretions
Masturbation frequency
Preferred forms of contraception
Variations in sexual responsiveness during the menstrual cycle
Attitudes about sexual freedom
Sexual feelings during pregnancy

Many other aspects of sexual behaviour and attitudes were sampled. Overall, it was intended to get a comprehensive picture of how a woman experiences the process of becoming sexually aroused. Special importance was attached to understanding her psychological feelings and reactions, since I felt that the psychological side of a woman's sexual responses had been neglected, with previous studies largely portraying arousal in mechanical, physiological terms. It should be incidentally mentioned, though, that physiological measures (for example, heart rate, vaginal temperature, stomach mobility) were also obtained under a variety of conditions (for example, while listening to an erotic story). The physiological findings are presented in *The Female Orgasm*.

Each woman's personality and life style were appraised with a range of psychological tests and questionnaires. This was done in order to see if her sexual behaviour related to the kind of person she is psychologically. Both conscious and unconscious attitudes were sampled. Projective psychological techniques like the Rorschach Ink Blot Test and the Thematic Apperception Test were employed. Also, there were batteries of procedures which made use of selective memory, responses to briefly exposed pictures, word associations, perception of spatial position, and so forth.

In order to look more closely at the question of how representative the women in the present study were, two aspects of their sexual behaviour were compared with the norms compiled by Kinsey, *et al.* (1953) from their much larger and diverse population of women. These comparisons were reassuring. The typical intercourse frequency per week in our samples was 3·4 and in the Kinsey samples it was 3·0. This is obviously a small difference. Similarly, about 38 per cent of the women in our study reported that they experience orgasm always or nearly always. The comparable Kinsey value for 42 per cent – which is also a minimal difference. In other ways too the two groups were found to be comparable in their sexual behaviour.

It should be specified that each woman's ability to reach orgasm was determined by asking her to respond to the following:

Circle the number that best completes the following statement as it applies to you:

During intercourse I experience orgasm:

Always	Nearly always	Frequently	Occasionally	Rarely	Never
1	2	3	4	5	6

It was established that responses to this inquiry were consistent and stable over a period of time. Furthermore, the orgasm self-ratings were found not to be correlated with formal psychological measures of the degree to which there is an intent to give a favourably biased impression of oneself. The women did not manipulate their ratings in order to present a biased or special image of their sexual prowess.

The average woman across the seven samples studied stated that she attains orgasm 'frequently'. Only about 39 per cent indicated that they achieve orgasm 'always' or 'nearly always'. In other words, for as much as 60 per cent of the women, orgasm did not occur consistently. About 5 or 6 per cent have never experienced orgasm at all. The average woman in the present studies attained her first marital orgasm within slightly more than two months of marriage. This is roughly comparable to the Kinsey, *et al.* observation that 55 per cent of their sample attained first marital orgasm by the end of the second month of marriage.

Negative Findings

A good deal that was uncovered by the experimental studies was as negative and unrevealing as had been the results when the existing scientific literature dealing with sexual responsiveness in women had been reviewed. It proved to be very difficult to show that a woman's ability to reach orgasm was due to specific, well-defined factors. The search for positive information turned out to be circuitous and tortuous, but I do not mean to depreciate the importance of the negative findings. They not only reinforced a number of the sceptical conclusions which had already been drawn from the review of the scientific literature, but also helped to narrow the regions in which potentially more positive studies could be undertaken.

A review and analysis of the negative findings follows.

Femininity

There are, of course, widely accepted popular assumptions about the role of 'femininity' in orgasmic response. It is thought that the more 'feminine' a woman is, the greater will be her orgasmic capacity. But in terms of the various formal measures of femininity used in the present studies, no support could be found for the notion. High- and low-orgasmic women did not differ in how closely their interest patterns conform to the accepted concepts of femininity. The woman whose pattern of interests resembles that of the average housewife was neither more nor less orgasmic than the woman whose patterns of interests resembles that of an engineer. High- and low-orgasmic women also did not differ in how interested they are in cosmetics, perfumes, new clothing fashions, and varied hair styles. In other words, a woman's orgasm consistency could not be estimated from the degree to which she lavishes 'beautifying' attention upon her body or makes use of perfume or seeks novelty in her appearance.

Early Dating Behaviour

Is the girl who begins to date early or who dates with relatively high frequency likely to become the woman who is especially orgasmic? In several groups of women information was obtained concerning dating behaviour in high school and college (for example, frequency, 'going steady'). Orgasmic capacity was found to be completely unrelated to the sheer quantity of dating or the frequency of intimate alliances designated by terms like 'going steady' and 'engaged'. It should be specified that no information was obtained concerning amount of premarital intercourse experience.

Psychological Disturbance

As pointed out earlier, there has been a strong inclination to link orgasm capacity with 'mental health'. Women who have difficulty in reaching orgasm are often regarded as psychologically maladjusted. In the present studies quite a variety of techniques were used to measure anxiety and psychological disturbance. They ranged from formal questionnaires to autobiographies to projective tests like the Rorschach. Furthermore, intensive interviews were held with many of the women which provided the opportunity to probe previous neurotic or psychotic symptoms. No consistent correlations between orgasm capacity and degree of disturbance could be established. Some of the most orgasmic women turned out to be people who were really very anxious and upset, while a number of the most unruffled and nonsymptomatic women were unable to reach orgasm at all. The tenor of these findings is in harmony with the earlier reviewed observations of other investigators, who also largely failed to see a tie between the state of a woman's mental health and her sexual responsiveness.

Religiosity

The women were asked to fill out a questionnaire in which they rated their own degree of religiosity and indicated not only their own frequency of church attendance but also that of their parents. Formal religious affiliation (for example, Catholic, Protestant, Jewish) was determined too. Once again the results were negative. Whether a woman is religiously devout or not is unrelated to her orgasm capacity. Whether a woman is Protestant, Catholic, or Jewish does not predict her sexual responsiveness. Just as was true in the Kinsey, *et al.* report, there is little evidence that religious factors play a prime part in whether a woman can build up orgasmic excitement.

Hostility and Dominance

Considerable information was gathered concerning both the overt and covert hostility of the women. Measures were derived from their responses to psychological tests and also their actual behaviour as observed by laboratory personnel. Relatedly, measures were obtained of how dominant versus submissive they were in their style of behaviour. This was done to see whether the hostile or dominant individual is less sexually responsive than the relatively non-hostile or submissive one. It was not possible to find any consistent relationships between a woman's orgasm capacity and the amount of hostility or need to dominate others detected in her. Angry women seem to be no more or less sexually responsive than those who display little anger. The 'pushy', dominating woman seems to be no more or less orgasmic that the acquiescent, submissive woman.

Clothing Preferences

One of the questions which was explored was whether women who differ in orgasm capacity differ in their attitudes toward clothing. Do they choose clothes from unlike perspectives or on the basis of unlike values? For example, does the high orgasmic woman exceed the low orgasmic one in choosing her clothing for its decorative, 'dress-up' impact or its conformity to style or its 'figure-revealing' qualities? A standardized questionnaire (Aiken, 1963) was used to measure clothing attitudes. It calls for true or false responses to such questions as the following:

I like close-fitting, figure-revealing dresses.
I approve of the Bikini bathing suit and wouldn't mind wearing one myself.
I buy dresses for comfort rather than appearance.

The clothing attitudes measured in this way proved to be unrelated to orgasm consistency.

Physique and Appearance

In several groups information was obtained from each woman concerning her developmental background and physique. She provided details concerning age at onset of menstruation, menstrual regularity, age at development of breasts and appearance of pubic hair, weight, height, dress size, breast size, and so forth. Each woman was also asked to judge her own physical attractiveness. Further, her attractiveness was rated by others in terms of personal observation and also pictures providing front and back views. Orgasm consistency was found to be unrelated to any of these measures. It is doubtful whether one can predict how orgasmic a woman will be from a knowledge of how early she developed secondary sex characteristics, the regularity of her menstrual cycle, or the size of her body. This is similarly true with respect to the attractiveness of her physical appearance, the size of her breasts, or her weight. It would appear that orgasmic capacity cannot be gauged from the obvious features of a woman's anatomy or physiological functioning. Other investigators like Terman (1951) and Landis (1940) have, with minor exceptions, come to essentially similar conclusions.

Parental Attitudes Towards Sex

Many inquiries were made concerning each woman's recall of her parents' attitudes toward sex. She was asked to judge how freely they had talked about sex and how approving or disapproving they were of sexual expression. She indicated too their attitude toward nudity; how reluctant they were to display affection; the ease or spontaneity with which they could physically touch her body. She described the nature of the sex education they had provided. Even further, she was asked to recall how they had responded at the time of her first menstrual period and her first serious date.

None of this information concerned with early sexual attitudes in the home turned out to be correlated with a woman's ability to reach orgasm. One woman who remembered her parents as extremely negative toward sexual expression was just as orgasmic as another who depicted her parents as very positive in this respect. Adequacy of early sex education was not correlated with orgasm capacity. Whether parents were pleased or shocked by the occurrence of their daughter's first menstrual period or her first serious encounter with boys did not foretell her likelihood of developing orgasm inhibitions. As seen through each woman's eyes, the atmosphere in her parental home with regard to the realm of sexuality did not seem to have much relevance for her later capacities to be sexually responsive.

Husband's Attitudes and Behaviour

All the women who were studied were married. Each was asked to provide detailed data about her husband's sexual behaviour, attitudes toward women, and other personality-related attributes. For example, she indicated his preferred frequency of intercourse, how often she felt it necessary to refuse his requests for intercourse, how much time he devoted to foreplay before beginning intercourse, and how easily she could discuss sexual matters with him. Also, she described how much they agreed or disagreed about many issues that confront married couples and the proper balance of husband-wife power in the family. She reported too whether she liked men to be aggressive and whether she considered men to be in a position to get more satisfaction from life than women do.

The yield from this appraisal was zero. None of the husband's attributes, as viewed by the wife, was linked with whether she could attain orgasm. A woman's orgasm capability was not related to whether she perceived her husband as too sexually demanding or overly aggressive or difficult to communicate with about sexual matters or limited in the amount of foreplay he provided. These findings were, of course, supportive of similar negative information about the husband's role in the wife's orgasm capacity which had been found in the earlier review of the scientific literature dealing with female sexuality.

To further demonstrate the similarities in the ways the high- and low-orgasmic women perceive their husbands, a series of representative excerpts will be presented of what women in each category said when they were asked to describe their husbands by speaking spontaneously into a tape recorder.

LOW ORGASM

Subject 1. My husband and I met in college when I was a freshman and he was a freshman . . . Actually, we didn't have any real serious problems that arose. It seemed to be – he told me when he saw me he realized that I was the girl for him. However, I didn't have this same feeling. I enjoyed going with him. We went to church together. We went to the matinée dances. We went to most of the activities together and had a good wholesome relationship. He's a very likeable person – not the tall, dark, and handsome type that my first boyfriend was but he has a very nice personality and anyone that even meets him now likes him and he gets along well with people. He has a good physical appearance . . . I guess the things that we have had the most difficulty in agreeing about could be maybe the discipline of our children and how we should work things out together before we actually have certain problems arise. We've never really had any financial disagreements with regard to the use of our money because we've always felt that this was something that was jointly ours and we have everything in common together with our banking and checking accounts together and our home, our car, everything we have we share together because we feel that this sort of a thing is important in a marriage, although we show him respect and he is the head of our household and he's the one who makes the final decisions.

Subject 2. Like I said, I met my husband when he was in the Army. I went to a dance and he was there and he asked me for a date and I accepted. I was very impressed with him. Up to that time I had just about made up my mind that there weren't many worthwhile men in this world but when I went home I told my cousin whom I was living with at this time that I finally met somebody that I think I could stand to be married to. When he got out of the Army – well, we were engaged – and then he got out of the Army . . . and we were married . . . We've had – at least from what I've seen – we have just about one of the happiest marriages that I've ever seen. We have our problems, of course. You just can't have two people living in a house together and not have problems, but we seem to be able to get most things straightened out. We've never had a fight; disagreements, yes, arguments, yes, and sometimes we get angry, but never a knock-down battle type of thing. He's a pretty calm person and he won't usually stand and argue with me. He'll just let me cool off and then he'll come back and talk about it later ... He's a very gentle person, very good to me. Gives me quite a bit of leeway to do just about what I want as long as I do the few things that he asks which is to keep up a neat home and cook his meals and take care of his clothes – I mean the things that any man would ask of a wife. He's very undemanding. He's very good with the children, very gentle and playful, and, in fact, they get all of the roughhouse and silly business with him more than from me. I think – it's a funny thing, too, but the things that we have the arguments about and the disagreements about are usually ways to handle the children, I guess.

Subject 3. I met my husband ... in college ... We didn't have very many dates as such; we didn't go to the movies or shows or to clubs or out to eat a lot. We did spend a great deal of time together, though, and although we only knew each other for about four months before we got married, I think we got to know each other quite well during that time. We listened to music a lot and we read sometimes and we went to a couple of plays, and I think we did a few oddball things ... Our courtship was short. He was proposing to me – I guess he started proposing to me about two months after we met, but I had been engaged the year before to another fellow and that had broken up, and I was still quite shy about getting involved again, so I kept saying no, although I did enjoy his company, but I didn't feel that I was quite ready to get married; I wanted to make certain that this was the right thing and it took a while. But when I finally did say yes, we were married shortly afterwards. The problems that arose were, I think, primarily financial. My husband was just a graduate student here and we knew things were going to be pretty rough financially when we got married, but we decided that we would go ahead and that we would make out. And we did ... I think my husband is handsome and I think he has a very nice personality. He's cheerful and he likes to make jokes quite often and wisecracks and puns, and I do too. He's very serious about his studies, which is one thing that I admire about him. I like a man that knows what he wants to do and goes ahead and does it.

Subject 4. As for my husband I met him at a party. Our courtship – well, I met him in June and we were married in November. About the biggest problem that arose, I would say, was the religious problem. He was Baptist at the time and I was Episcopalian ... There was a little disagreement here, but we did compromise ... My husband, as far as his physical appearance, is tall ... and a very nice built man, neat in his appearance. As for his personality, he's very friendly and honest and kind.

Subject 5. My husband – I had met him – he ate in the same restaurant where I did . . . and I used to date his cousin but our courtship really didn't start until our senior year . . . He asked me to a basketball game . . . He got serious and all of a sudden we were going together, the next thing you know. Problems: well, we didn't have any problem with religion because he never pushed it. He just said, well, you know I'd have to sign a paper but he didn't care whether I converted or not, and I think because of the fact that he took a completely hands-off attitude, that's why I was able to be interested in it because he never let religion come into our relationship as a boy and girl, so we never had discussions or fights or anything over that and it never got involved with the two of us personally so that any decision that I made was my own rather than something connected with being in love and so on. Problems that arose mostly were with my family. They didn't care too much for him, to say the least – him or his religion both – they don't like him personally. And I thought we got along all right, though I never thought he was perfect and I realized that he was not the warmest personality in the world, not the – well – kind to think of other people first, let me put it that way . . . And personality-wise, he's kind of erratic. He's either very voluble and excitable or else he's completely dead to the world.

HIGH ORGASM

Subject 1. I met my husband on a blind date. His room-mate was engaged to my cousin. He was – let's see – he was really kind of fun on that first night. It was a rainy night; we went to the movies and walked all the way downtown; there were no buses running; and from that time on I think I only had one other date with another fellow and he never dated another girl after we started going together. We got engaged eight months later but didn't get married until over a year later . . . He's a very easygoing fellow, although sometimes it irritates him when people take advantage of him but I think he lets them take advantage of him a lot of the time. He likes to do outside reading, although he doesn't seem to get much time to do it. He likes to work with people. He's always been fairly liberal politically but I think he's changing somewhat, although he denies this. He was raised in a very strict home . . . and until he was in high school he never went to movies and his family forbade drinking or smoking – anything like that. The only problem that we had during the courtship was over religion. He was much more religious than I was. I hadn't been to church in ages and didn't have any plans for going to church regularly. I think we agreed on our philosophy toward religion and it was just the practice that we didn't agree on. I never seemed to practise very much and that was the one problem.

Subject 2. I met my husband in Texas where he was stationed. I met him at a party . . . We didn't know each other very long. We knew each other about five months, and we got married. We had relations before we got married. The only problem I have ever had is that I get very, very jealous and he is just the opposite . . . He is very egotistical. He gets along well with children. The only arguments we ever have are about him not spending enough time with his family because it's school, baseball games, etc., etc. But we've ironed those out pretty well. Personality-wise: everyone seems to like him. He's very sarcastic – the two of us are when we get together; we're very, very sarcastic with each other but mainly because there's someone else around. He is not a very romantic fellow. He's not one to put his – to say I love you once in a while – it's a very seldom thing. Really the most important thing that my husband and I have difficulty in agreeing about is how to discipline the children and we still haven't ironed that one out yet.

Subject 3. I met my husband through a friend of mine . . . We corresponded . . . and talked about a lot of lovely, unrealistic, rosy, romantic things which we saw eye to eye on in many ways . . . We really didn't know each other too well when we married. He made me uneasy in many ways but I felt very strongly that this was something that I should do. He was a good person and a very brilliant person. All in all, I think I made a very wise choice. He's not the most beautiful person in the world but he's not an ugly person. He's rather an appealing person. I think his personality probably makes him more appealing, although he is rather shy and in some instances he has an awful lot of finesse. Most of the time he gets along very well with people at work, with everybody but me, it seems . . . He's a kind person and believes that kindness is better than gruffness. He likes things quiet and relaxed and not demanding and not pushing. Both of us are quite within ourselves in many ways and definitely – he's definitely not an extrovert but he's not an introvert and he's quite a bright person, in my viewpoint.

Subject 4. I met him at a party. He was quiet, reserved . . . We started to date and continued for quite a while. I don't remember agreeing about much; I just remember disagreeing about a lot of things. I was very religious at this time and he wasn't, we disagreed about religion. And, oh, he used to go with a girl . . . and he always seemed to be flirting with her and we disagreed about that quite a bit. And I guess we didn't agree very much the first time. We broke up after four months because I felt he was flirting with the other girl too much one night and then I started to go with him again . . . And he didn't realize it, but I was chasing him. I was quite subtle about it. I knew how to get around him and I still do sometimes. And I snagged him again and we went together for a while and then we broke up because he was such a creep . . . But somehow we got back together again and I really don't remember what we disagreed about or agreed about. We just disagreed about all kinds of things. I guess I'm describing my husband and my courtship. Problems that arose: we had all kinds of problems but none of them were really that serious . . . He's relatively quiet with strangers. He's become much more outgoing in the years that I have known him. His mother seems to think that I've been a very good influence because he used to be very unsociable and very reserved, but now he enjoys people, he enjoys being with a group and he's usually quite good in a group, particularly if it's a relatively well-educated group . . .

Subject 5. I met my husband in college. It was a light relationship at first and all the way, on my part. I think to a great extent I was merely having fun . . . He is pleasant looking. His personality is that of a good person. He's decent and honourable. He enjoys sports a great deal – working on mechanical things. He enjoys animals and the outdoors, children. He wants to have a good job, a nice home, good family. His personality and mental make-up do not run deep but he is a very loyal person and a very dependable person. So this, to an extent, compensates for his lack of aesthetic training and self-expression on subjects which are closer to my heart and to my interests than physical activity.

A thorough analysis of these and other tape-recorded descriptions of the husband did not reveal the slightest difference between the high- and low-orgasmic women.

Attitudes Towards Sex

Do high- and low-orgasmic women differ in their stated views about the importance of sex in one's life? Do they show contrasting feelings about sexual satisfaction? Do they assign different meanings or significance to sexuality? From the questionnaire and interview material we obtained, one would have to answer these questions negatively. There were no obvious differences in sexual attitudes between these classes of women. The similarities in their stated perspectives on the world of sex can be vividly communicated by means of the following representative excerpts from what they had to say about sex when asked to freely express themselves on this topic by spontaneous talk.

LOW ORGASM

Subject 1. Concerning my attitudes toward love, sex, and the expression of sexual feelings, I feel that my whole outlook stems from the fact that I was brought up in a home without any brothers or without a father and it has been stressed to me over and over again that the important thing about our life is that we should have children and that's our purpose. So perhaps my own feeling and attitude is brought about by this and maybe it is a little off-balance in the fact that my mother was alone and without a husband for so long and she felt that she could do without this sexual experience of a husband and perhaps her attitudes and ideas have rubbed off on to me, that I can take it or leave it. Actually, I could probably go on and on and on without a sexual act. I don't have that great of a desire for sexual intercourse and many times I feel that I am inadequate to my husband because of this and I wish that I did have stronger sexual feelings. However, I do love my husband greatly and I like to embrace him and I want him to kiss me and love me but I don't feel that I respond and take the initiative in these acts in our intimate feeling together as I should. Sometimes I think that I'm just a cold cucumber but I try to show warmth and love and understanding toward my husband, and I feel perhaps when we were first married I did this more so than I do now and other things have sort of taken the place of this, perhaps my attention and feelings toward my children. But I think we have to broaden ourselves so that we can take them into our lives and still not neglect our husbands. However, I feel that sex, as I stated before, is not the ultimate that we're here for and, of course, this also comes out of our religious training and background. We're here to prove ourselves, to see if we'll choose right and do the things that our Father in Heaven wants us to do and rearing a family and having children is part of this experience and our ultimate goal is to so live that we might have our children and our family eternally, that even though we die we'll still have our husbands and our children in the next world and forever.

Subject 2. I think sex can be a very lovely thing in its place and it belongs with married people and nowhere else. I believe that it isn't only for having children. Of course, it's very necessary for bringing children into the world for people to have sexual relations but I think it can be a builder in your marriage. I think it draws you together and I think that when people start degrading it and making dirty remarks about it, it makes me angry because I don't think it's the sort of thing to poke fun at. I think they act like little kids – you know, when they giggle about things. I don't think people like that are grown-up when they start making these silly remarks and telling silly jokes. I have a very strong feeling of the home with people being married and rearing families. I don't see how society can exist without it and I feel badly when I hear people talking about – oh, you hear weird ideas of people about free-love type of thing where men and women can just live together and no responsibility, no ties. I think they've lost the whole meaning of sex. I think it's overrated on one side and underrated on another. I think it's just a normal, natural thing that people should come to accept and enjoy and quit talking about it. I've never felt embarrassed toward my husband. I've never felt embarrassed about anything we've done together. I never will because he's my husband and it's natural. And this is the thing that I hope to imbue in my children to help them to accept it as just a natural, normal, happy thing that belongs in a certain place.

Subject 3. My attitudes about love, sex and the expression of sexual feelings I would say are quite normal. It's certainly right to express your sexual feelings to your partner – your husband or wife – and I think that people should not be timid about this. Love certainly is a very important part of life. It is throughout the animal kingdom, and there's no reason why it should be repressed. I don't think that people should think that it's dirty or anything like that. It's perfectly natural and very important and very enjoyable. I think, on the whole, I feel very happy about love and sex and the expression of sexual feelings.

Subject 4. As far as summarizing my attitudes toward love, sex, and the expression of sexual feelings, well, my attitudes toward love, as far as a husband and wife relationship is, as I said before, it's just a compassion, a genuine concern and care for the one you love, caring how he feels when he's hurt, whether he feels good or bad or happy or sad, sharing your life together, raising your children together, bringing them up in as happy a home as possible where there's love and devotion and goodness. As far as my attitudes toward sex, summarizing them, I would say somewhere along the way I got a very mixed-up feeling on sex. I know as a young girl when I was dating, I always enjoyed going out and, well – what would you call it – making out after a date, just kissing and maybe light petting – I know I enjoyed this. However, I believe I was not educated on sex the way I should have been, otherwise I may have had a different outlook on it, I don't know. Right now I know I am depriving my husband of a lot in our marriage because I just don't know how to help myself want sex more. I would like to be loving and feel and enjoy sex and experience orgasm which I don't believe – maybe I have once or twice within the last year. I just wish I could be a better sexual partner to my husband. As far as sexual feelings, well, I would say again when I was younger, during my teenage years, perhaps when I had steady boyfriends and when I was engaged the one time, I did enjoy sexual feelings . . . I don't know – as far as sexual feelings I'm very, very mixed up. I would say to summarize that it is of great importance to be told what is expected in life, to be told when one is developing and growing into maturity what is happening to their body, that it is nothing to be afraid of or embarrassed of, that it is just natural, that sex is nothing to be afraid of or embarrassed about or to feel wrongly about, that it is really a beautiful part of love and marriage.

Subject 5. Well, I think I have a pretty healthy attitude toward love and sex and the expression of sexual feelings – a lot healthier than my husband. He has some kind of a problem along that line. But I – as I say, I'm not unconventional as to how to do it. I mean, I like one standard position, all the standard things – I'm not an experimenter, shall we say. I guess that's the end of it.

HIGH ORGASM

Subject 1. I think as far as love, sex, and the expression of sexual feelings go, I'm a very moral person. I believe that sex should be restricted to a married couple, and I think that if it is, there's a real warmth of having one partner that you love very much and who understands you and whom you know, and saving this for just this one person as something very special that you don't do with anyone else.

Subject 2. Love, sex, and the expression of sexual feelings. I think it's fine. I am very romantic. I like sex. I like intercourse, I mean. I enjoy it. I think the most wonderful thing that ever happened to me was when I got married. I don't know what I'd say about my attitudes on the expression of sexual feelings. I'm free. I do whatever I feel like doing. Anything that would make my husband happy is fine with me. There are a few things I don't like but – I don't know. I don't know whether to say anything more. I think I've talked about everything that's on the papers and – let's see. I guess that's all.

Subject 3. How would I summarize my attitudes toward love, sex, and the expression of sexual feelings? I like it. Even though my husband and I fight about it. We do have different views. I am not a cold person. Sometimes I feel very dumb and I don't think we need to have intercourse as often as we do sometimes, and sometimes it's the method in which it is approached that bothers me. But love is a warm feeling and it is a trusting and it's being able to open up and be yourself without getting your feelings hurt or crushed or criticized. I think love is accepting one another, what they believe, and I think sex is an expression of this love and can be a very satisfying thing and can be a release of emotions and tension, and I think it brings a husband and wife closer together and should be done only in love, not to settle arguments, although it can be a help in this area. And I think if you feel you need to express yourself sexually you should feel free to do so as long as it doesn't embarrass or injure the feelings or physical being of your partner. And that's – I hope that's satisfactory. I have lots more to say but I've run out of time.

Subject 4. My attitudes toward love, sex, and the expression of sexual feelings. Fine. I think love is great and sex is great and the expression of sexual feelings is great. I feel they're healthy and natural and I certainly enjoy them and I think I will continue to for the rest of my life.

Subject 5. My attitudes toward love, sex, and the expression of sexual feelings. I believe in the great power of love toward the achievement of happiness. Simple good feelings between people can do more to advance our civilization in the most important way – not in the sense of technical advancement or scientific discovery. I think that just a general social concern and sensitivity between people is the most important thing we should be working toward at this time before we get to the moon. Sex is an enjoyable and a very transcendent act. It, I think, is one of the closest acts that we have to nature. I don't agree with the role it has been forced to take as something forbidden, something to be snickered at – we have in the books and the movies and the records. I think it should be put on a higher plane than our society puts it, but this, of course, has to begin between two people. It starts in the intimacy between two people and their attitude toward what they're feeling. I think that the individual can influence society – not necessarily the society influencing the individual in all cases. And I personally would like to see sexuality put on a level of appreciation as we place beautiful artistic endeavours, beautiful music, literary expression, because it is an elevating thing. It is something that takes us away from the banality of everyday activity and simple earthly thoughts. It is something that could almost be looked upon with a religious attitude – a sort of a reverence and a deep appreciation that it is available to us – sexual fulfillment and emotional development and expansion, achievement in the sense of loving and communicating this love to a whole family that you have produced – to whole humanity in which you live, I think, can be the greatest thing that we could achieve.

Other Negative Findings

Many other negative results, too numerous to describe in detail, were accumulated. I will only list a relatively few of special interest.

Orgasm consistency was found to be unrelated to how exhibitionistic a woman is or how much she seeks attention. The person who is quiet and shy may be just as sexually responsive as the one who is 'loud' and displays herself.

The orderly, well-controlled woman seems to be just as orgasmic as the impulsive, 'sloppy' one. Relatedly, the woman who enjoys quiet routine was no less orgasmic than the woman who likes variety and adventure.

The 'conservative' woman (as defined by a formal measure of political attitudes) is as sexually responsive as the 'liberal' one. This applies also to the distinction between women who have conservative as compared to liberal attitudes about what is proper or acceptable social behaviour.

There is evidence that the woman who is interested in achievement and 'getting ahead' does not differ in her orgasmic potential from the one who is passive and uninterested in accomplishment.

Note further that high- and low-orgasmic women do not differ significantly with respect to:

their amount of interest in sports
how much they smoke
how much alcohol they consume
how happy they consider their parents' marriage to be
their habitual degree of cheerfulness, friendliness, and desire to help others
how dependent and 'weak' they feel
their degree of investment in being nurturant or 'maternal'
their usual amount of pain and discomfort during menstruation
how masochistic or self-depreciating they are in their orientation
their usual level of guilt and sense of not being 'up to standard'
how satisfied and secure they feel about their body

Comments

The task of pinpointing by means of experimental studies the kinds of personal qualities that are correlated with differences in ability to respond consistently to orgasm proved in many ways to be an elusive one. There are so many things with which orgasm consistency is not linked! Particularly noteworthy is the fact that it does not seem to be related to maladjustment or psychological disturbance, at least in the sense that such terms are conventionally understood. This is congruent with the conclusion earlier reached, based on a review of the empirical literature concerned with sexual responsiveness in women, that there does not appear to be a relationship between the 'mental health' of a woman and her ability to attain orgasm. To know that a woman is unusually tense or even unusually anxious does not predict her orgasm capacity.

Another stereotype which has been challenged by the present

findings is that orgasmic ability is somehow a derivative of a woman's degree of 'femininity'. No correlations of significance have been obtained between orgasm consistency and various standard measures of femininity. One cannot judge a woman's orgasm capacity in terms of how interested she is in 'feminine' things or endorses values customarily considered to be womanly. It is pertinent that no differences could be detected between high- and low-orgasmic women with reference to their attitudes towards clothes, use of cosmetics, or other aspects of personal adornment. Further, judges who carefully studied pictures in which the appearance and dress style of a sample of women could be observed did no better than chance in deciding how orgasmic they were. It will be recalled, in this same vein, that orgasm consistency was unrelated to such actual physical parameters as a woman's height, weight, breast size, age she began to menstruate, and so forth. It was also unrelated to how much she enjoys physical activity as indicated by her frequency of participation in sports. In short, there does not seem to be any way of predicting how orgasmic a woman will be on the basis of information about her appearance and other physical attributes or the manner in which she treats and adorns her body or the speed with which her body developed secondary sex characteristics.

A salient negative finding is the fact that a woman's orgasm consistency is unrelated to how friendly or unfriendly, hostile or non-hostile, she is. This was found to be true despite the fact that an unusually serious attempt was made to evaluate each woman's hostility characteristics comprehensively. An inclusive repertoire of procedures was utilized which measured overt friendliness (as judged by observers), self-rated friendliness, and amount of hostile feeling and also hostile fantasy. The findings obtained suggest that a woman's habitual level of anger and her style of coping with anger do not play a role in orgasm consistency. As noted earlier, one cannot tell from a woman's degree of aggressiveness or dominance whether she has high or low orgasm capacity. Analogously, women scoring high on sociability, cheerfulness, and desire to help others do not differ in orgasmic capacity from those who score low on such variables.

One cannot foretell a woman's orgasm consistency from how

'free' or impulsive or emotional she is. Orgasm consistency did not differ for women who make decisions slowly and carefully as contrasted to those who respond quickly, on the spur of the moment. It did not differ for those who prefer a constricted, safe, unexciting style of life as compared to those who constantly seek excitement and new adventure. Orgasmic capacity seems to have little to do with a woman's conventionality or unconventionality. The woman whose interest patterns resemble those of the typical housewife is just as likely to be orgasmic as the woman whose interests are more unique or exotic. Apropos of this matter of conventionality, it will be recalled, too, that religiosity and church attendance were not correlated with orgasm capacity. In fact, the extremeness of a woman's beliefs about sexual freedom seem unrelated to the orgasm index. High- and low-orgasmic women do not differ in their opinions about how much sexual freedom there should be or the manner in which sex education should be given. Tangential to this point, it is also interesting that they do not differ in terms of how permissive they recall their parents to have been about sexual matters (for example, talking freely about sex or permitting body exposure in the home). The woman who perceives her parents as having been puritanical about sex is just as likely to be consistently orgasmic as the woman who characterizes her parents as extremely liberal about sex! Of course, this finding clashes with most accepted views concerning this matter. It is almost a truism in the clinical literature that parents who are narrow and secretive about sex will produce sexual dysfunction in their children. The data from the present study raise doubt about complacently accepting such a dictum. Indeed, one is reminded at this point that religiosity and church attendance, which might be regarded as roughly indicative of degree of acceptance of puritanical standards about sex, have not been reliably linked with orgasm consistency either in the present study or in the Kinsey, *et al.* (1953) surveys.

It should be noted too that there is no evidence that orgasm capacity occurs more often in the dramatic, adventurous, emotional woman than in the conventional, timid, orderly woman. A woman's ability to attain orgasm is apparently not defined by such stylistic elements.

The negative findings just reviewed were almost always in the forefront of those spelled out by the computer to which the experimental data were submitted for analysis. However, in the next chapter we shall describe the first thread of positive and integrating continuity that began to show itself as further lines of investigation were undertaken.

4. *Orgasm Capacity and the Loss of Love*

Despite the disappointing and surprisingly negative results of our review of research, which I have described, I felt convinced that there must be some distinctive theme or life orientation which plays a significant role in whether a woman can muster orgasmic excitement. None of the expected 'explanations' of female orgasm differences seemed to hold up. Yet there had to be some explanation. We decided to look for clues to a possible solution in the various kinds of fantasy material which we had obtained from the women. I searched particularly in the images evoked by the Rorschach Ink Blots. Each woman had been asked to look at the blots and to give imaginative interpretations of what they might represent. Gradually, as I was scanning the responses of high- and low-orgasmic women in one sample we had collected, I began to detect a trend which suggested that the low-orgasmic women seemed to be more preoccupied with images of death. More than other women, they seemed to be concerned with the themes related to death and to loss of loved ones through death. They produced an unusual number of such images as the following: 'dead body', 'graveyard', 'ghost', 'funeral hearse'. When I formally checked this observation in several other samples of women we had studied, there was a consistent, quantitatively demonstrable trend for death imagery to occur with relatively greater frequency among the low- as compared to the high-orgasmic women. The results were solid and convincing. My overall interpretation was that the woman with orgasm difficulties is inwardly more concerned with the uncertain, nondependable character of her relationships. That is, she doubts the permanence of things – especially of her relationships with the important figures in her life.

Reinforcement for the findings concerning loss appeared when an analysis was undertaken of imaginative stories which the women had created both spontaneously and in response to various pictures. It was found that the greater a woman's preoccupation in her stories with themes of loss and separation the less was her orgasm capacity. The nature or flavour of the difference between the high- and low-orgasm women can best be conveyed by comparing two typical stories, one created by a high- and the other by a low-orgasmic woman. Both of these stories were given in response to the instruction to make up a story about a 'girl and her mother'. The high-orgasmic woman responded as follows:

A girl and her mother did lots of things together. They went shopping and took trips together. They shared funny stories and humour together. They were sensitive to each other and they looked like each other. Many people who didn't know the mother but knew the girl said to the mother, when they saw her, that they knew she was the girl's mother just by looking at her.

The low-orgasmic woman said:

The girl and her mother had grown very close over the years. There had been many rugged times when the mother had to work hard to keep her daughter, as she (the daughter) was asthmatic and constantly ill. The father had left to seek greener and younger pastures and so the mother had full responsibility for caring for the ill girl and supporting her. At one period the child was so sick that she could do nothing but vomit for a period of twenty-four hours and the mother had to work all day and sit with her child all night. There were several days like this and the mother became weak with fatigue. She had to send her child to a home where they could care for her professionally so she could keep her job. The girl cried and was unhappy but still knew her mother loved her and understood.

One can see in these examples that while the mother and daughter are said to have a close relationship in both instances, it eventually turns out in the story of the low-orgasm woman that mother and daughter become separated because the mother 'had to send her child to a home'. That is, despite the mother's apparent loving attitude she has to turn her daughter over to others and no longer are they together.

There were also other ways in which the differential concern about separation and loss showed up. One group of women were asked to think back and recall events that had occurred in their childhood. When these early memories were examined, it was found that the low-orgasmic more often than the high-orgasmic focused on the losses they had suffered in childhood. They were more likely to recall the death of a relative or of a favourite pet. Even more impressive was the fact that when the autobiographies of a sample of women were analysed, it was found that the high- and low-orgasmic women differed significantly in how available a father had been to them during childhood. The low-orgasmic were more likely to say that they could not set up a relationship with the father either because he had died early or was absent from home for long periods as a consequence of his work. They portrayed the father as someone who had slipped away from them. Interestingly, they did not differ from the high-orgasmic in how frequently they described the mother as unavailable for a solid relationship. This is an interesting fact and more will be said about it later.

Overall, there was enough converging evidence to suggest that a woman's ability to reach orgasm is tied to her feelings about loss. Apparently, the more she feels that you cannot depend on being able to hold on to the people and things you value, the more limited is her orgasm capacity. The question immediately arises as to the way in which concern about loss might interfere with orgasm. The key to answering this question may be the blurring of perception that occurs in the average woman as sexual excitement builds and she approaches orgasm. Kinsey, *et al.* (1953) have described the decrease in sensory sharpness that accompanies sexual arousal. Vision becomes blurred and at the point of orgasm there may even be momentary loss of consciousness. In other words, the outer world becomes somewhat vague; and objects are simply less distinctly perceived. It is this fading of objects which may disturb the woman who is already oversensitized to the possibility of losing or being separated from her supports. She may regard the perceptual 'loss' of objects during her sexual arousal as akin to the loss she has chronically expected to plague her. Therefore, she reacts with alarm to her slipping 'hold' on things during intercourse; and this alarm interferes with her becoming sufficiently further aroused to reach orgasm. She cannot be receptive to sexual stimulation which carries her too far along the excitement trajectory away from clear contact with the world. This is one of the major ideas that emerged from our studies of the orgasm experience. It needs to be further verified, but meanwhile it provides a framework for looking scientifically at the nature of orgasm difficulties in the female.

It is an interesting sidelight that in a group of pregnant women who were studied, the relationship between orgasm capacity and concern about loss was revealed in the way the delivery was viewed. The whole process of delivery represents an event of dramatic proportions, confronting a woman with the need to adapt as an individual to difficult stress. It is particularly likely to churn up feelings about loss and aloneness. Typically, the woman who is about to deliver is brought into an alien hospital environment, separated from her husband, and called upon to adapt to painful events with only one familiar face (that of her obstetrician) in view. One might expect that the woman with low-orgasm consistency would be particularly threatened by being placed in such a situation. Exploration of this possibility was carried out by asking a series of pregnant women to write detailed descriptions of their delivery experiences (as soon after the delivery as possible). The descriptions were analysed and tabulations made of all statements indicating concern about being alone or deserted or ignored. It turned out that the lower a woman's orgasm consistency, the more likely she was to express feelings of having been deserted and left alone by her obstetrician and the hospital personnel.

It would be well to summarize what has been presented. Making use of fantasy material and self-reports, it was possible to demonstrate in various ways that women with low- versus high-orgasm consistency differ in their preoccupation with themes of death and loss and also in amount of concern about being alone and deserted. The low-orgasm woman exceeds the high-orgasm woman in projecting death themes into her ink-blot interpretations; depicting characters in her fictional stories as likely to become estranged and separated; perceiving her father as unavailable for a close relationship during the early years; recalling her childhood as a time of loss of significant figures; and feeling deserted and alone after entering the hospital to have her child delivered. One of the most obvious ways of interpreting these findings is in terms of the idea that the low-orgasm woman feels insecure about the dependability of relationships. She could be said to expect that those she loves will die or leave or become separated from her. It is as if she assumed that union with someone else could not be counted upon to persist, but rather to be terminated unexpectedly. In essence, then, she might be said to view herself as lacking *dependable* attachment to people who really count. Her anxiety about loss may then get converted into real alarm when, in the course of building up sexual excitement, she finds that objects become perceptually hazy and seem to be 'slipping away'. The fading of objects signifies losing them and she cannot tolerate such loss. Her alarm interferes with the process of accumulating enough excitement to reach orgasm.

Endurance

Other interesting results having to do with orgasm were also obtained. One has to do with a personality difference between high- and low-orgasmic women. A formal personality measure (Edwards Personal Preference Schedule) was administered to several samples of women and a dimension called Endurance proved to be reliably linked with orgasm consistency. This dimension refers to how well an individual can keep at a job until it is finished; how hard he works at tasks; how likely he is to stick at a problem even though progress is slow. It was found that the higher a woman's Endurance score the greater was her orgasm consistency. This means that the more a woman can stick to a task and persist in dealing with a problem even in the face of complication or interruption the greater is her orgasm consistency. It may not be far fetched to see a link between this finding and that involving the correlation between orgasm consistency and concern about loss. Perhaps the woman who sticks to a task, persisting even in the face of complication and interruption, has a basic trust that her efforts will, in the long run, be rewarded. Presumably, her persistence reflects confidence in the trustworthiness of the world and a feeling that it can be depended upon to give a return if effort is invested in it. One could say that the woman with high orgasm consistency who believes in the reliability of objects and relationships expresses this orientation in her willingness to persist at tasks which she assumes will be ultimately rewarding. But the low orgasm woman who doubts the permanence of objects would have less reason to expect that persistent efforts would have a real pay-off. Another point relevant to the matter of Endurance anticipates some information which will be presented in detail later. When women were asked to describe their intercourse experiences, many emphasized that in order to reach orgasm they had to exclude outside stimuli which might be distracting and there had to be an intense, unwavering concentration on one's own body and the sensations produced by sexual stimulation. This could be interpreted to mean that the attainment of orgasm requires, to some degree, the ability to persist or concentrate, even if distractions occur. One could say that reaching orgasm demands of a woman that she be able to persist in a build-up process despite momentary disappointments, distractions, and downward shifts in arousal.

Relationship With Father

Another important finding concerns the way in which an individual was treated during childhood. In several samples of women a questionnaire was administered which probed their memories of how their mothers and fathers typically behaved. It was found with reliable consistency that the lower a woman's orgasm capacity the more likely she is to describe her father as having treated her 'casually', without elaborate attempts at control or enforcing his will, informally, and easy-going rather than expecting conformity to well-defined rules. To put it another way, the greater a woman's orgasm capacity, the less permissive and the more controlling she perceives her father to be. When this finding first emerged, I was surprised. There is little in the past literature dealing with the sexual behaviour of women which would prepare one for the possibility that the strict, controlling father is more likely than the casual permissive father to 'produce' a daughter who easily attains orgasm. But what if this finding is viewed against the background of the link between orgasm consistency and fear concerning the lack of dependability of relationships? Is it possible that the father of the low-orgasm daughter by acting casual and permissive toward her and not expecting her to live up to a fairly well-defined and enforced code of rules gives her a feeling that their relationship is tenuous? Is his casual attitude interpreted as a lack of solid commitment to the relationship? The temptation to answer this question affirmatively is increased if one looks closely at the kinds of questions which each woman who was studied had to answer about her father. A woman who depicted her father as clearly casual and not interested in setting definite standards would need to agree with the following statements applied to his mode of dealing with her before she had reached the age of twelve.

He let me spend my money any way I liked.
He let me stay up as late as I liked.
He let me do pretty much what I wanted to do.
He did not tell me what time to be home when I went out.
He did not bother much about making rules stick.

Some of this behaviour on a father's part could be viewed as thinly separated from indifference and lack of genuine concern about his daughter's welfare.

The difference in the way the high- and low-orgasmic women view the father can perhaps be even better conveyed by quoting in detail what they said when they were asked to speak into a tape recorder and give a word portrait of him. The following are some representative excerpts of these descriptions:

LOW ORGASMIC

Subject 1. There's not much I can describe or say about my father, having never known him except for the things that my mother has told me about him. And I'm sure that I was envious of other children who did have fathers and I didn't, and it sort of was a joke that my mother would say to me, 'Well, you find someone that you like for a father. You pick him out and we'll see what we can do.' However, I know from my mother's attitude how much she had loved my father and there was just never another man that could take his place. And she was never interested in anyone else.

Subject 2. My father, like I say, was in the Army . . . I don't know whether he enjoyed his Army life or not. I suspect that in the beginning he did but he grumbled a lot about it. But then that doesn't always necessarily mean that a person doesn't like it. I think sometimes grumbling with him was just a habit because he grumbled about everything. As far as beliefs, he talked a lot about being honest and about not stealing or lying or cheating people, although he was never honest – as I got older I realized that he wasn't even honest with himself. Maybe he didn't even know it, I don't know. He was very dictatorial. He was usually kind to me. I only remember one spanking I ever got. The things that he did were all emotional. He was so strict and sometimes unreasonable and sometimes he would tell you that you could do something and then five minutes before you got ready to go he'd change his mind, and you never got an explanation for it, but his only explanation for it was, 'I said so, therefore that's the way it is' . . . He drank quite heavily and life was really pretty miserable when he was around . . . He just drank all the time and was quite brutal – not to me but to my mother . . . I enjoyed school and I didn't particularly enjoy being around him. He seemed to have – oh, faith in me. He was proud of me. I could tell this. Whenever I did anything that he especially liked he always bragged about it to his friends and always introduced me to people that he brought around. I really think he could have been a very nice person if he hadn't had this drinking problem, but when he was doing that he wasn't even worth being around.

Subject 3. My father is – I would say he is a rather unusual person. He is quite intelligent; he has many, many talents – probably too many for his own good. His interests and work vary from time to time. He went to drama school. He was also a motorcycle and car racer, mechanic, and an engineer. He had a home-repair shop for many years and he really excelled with this . . . I think he was a bit selfish in that his interests came before the interest of his family, and I think that affected his relationship with my mother and with the children. He's a very flamboyant character. He drinks a great deal; as a matter of fact, he's an alcoholic and probably has been for many years and now, because of that, he finds it difficult to hold a job. He's usually quite cheerful; he likes to tell jokes; at least he's cheerful on the outside – I don't know how he feels on the inside. I respect his intelligence; I respect his talents; and when I was younger he took a great deal of interest in my talents and abilities and he tried to work with me in these. He had me take flute lessons for years, and I think I did quite well at it. I know I wouldn't have if he didn't take the interest in that. He also was interested in my art work, and I think I sort of inherited a little bit of his mechanical skill, although not nearly as much as he has. He's really a very colourful character.

Subject 4. Now to describe my father. Well, he was a very good-natured man. He drank a lot; in fact, I'd say he was an alcoholic. He had many different jobs as far back as I can remember, one after another. We lived with my aunt until I was sixteen years old and then my mother and father, my brother and I moved to an apartment. My father had no particular interests, I don't believe, except drinking, although he was a very kind and good-natured man and I loved him very much. His work: he was a mechanic and he worked for many different garages here in the city . . . He never went to church, as far as I can remember, but I do remember him talking about God and things. Problems: well, his problems were drinking. As far as his relationship with me, I would say we had a good relationship. I can remember as a little girl I was always happy with him but embarrassed when I saw him coming home drunk or if he took me out some place while he was drinking. But later on after he became ill and stopped drinking . . . I felt very sorry for him; he could not work any more. All he did was sit at home and watch television and he seemed to enjoy just staying at home. And, as I say, we were friendly and I know my father loved me as I loved him. I would not say we were very close as far as carrying on a conversation with each other to any extent, but just a comfortable relationship.

Subject 5. My father's main characteristic was that he was an alcoholic and naturally didn't make things too pleasant in the home and didn't do anything for our relationship. His work: he was an architect and he was pretty good in his work, but if he hadn't been good he never would have stayed on his job because he was always sleeping it off and not going in and so on. He wasn't religious; I don't believe he had any – I don't know whether he believed in God or not, to tell the truth. He never went to church or anything. I suppose he must have believed in something. Well, his problems were whatever made him drink and then the problems resulting from that, of course, didn't do anything for his marriage relationship or any other kind of relationship. He always made a big thing about how I was supposed to – well, first of all, he was always saying how I was planned – I wasn't an accident and then he wanted me to be a boy and he was always trying to – as if he never knew who I was. He was always acting as if I was a boy and he seemed to think I should be interested in engineering and mechanical things which I had not the slightest aptitude for and he was always – on the rare occasions when he did want to be nice I think he couldn't understand why my mother and I and my brother didn't just turn into the big happy family, but you just don't forget things overnight. So I wouldn't say that we had a particularly good relationship but then there could be worse, I'm sure, because if it hadn't been for the drinking he wouldn't have been too bad a person. As far as discipline and so on is concerned I don't think we had any problem there. I mean whatever I did was never good enough; no matter what grades I got, why, he thought I should have something better, but then he always went and bragged to everybody else about how good I was, so he was kind of two-faced about that.

HIGH ORGASMIC

Subject 1. My father is a fairly elderly person . . . And he worked for a large company all of his life since I remember him . . . He's the sort of person that likes to do work around the house. We had a fairly large home and on weekends he would always be out in the summer, painting or cutting the hedge or mowing the lawn, or doing some kind of work to keep the house up. He was very meticulous about the way the place looked. Everything had to be painted before it got to look bad and the lawn always had to look nice – weeds out and things like that. He liked to play golf. He used to play once a week and when I was little before we had a television set, he used to come home and spend most of the evening reading the newspaper or magazines or something like this. Later, when we got the television when I was about eight, he spent a fair amount of time watching the television at night. I think he's a very – a terribly conservative person in his beliefs. He was born in Scotland and . . . was in the First World War and then he moved to the United States where he met my mother. My father always expected a lot from his children, to the point where I think he was almost blind to some of our faults, and if you ever mentioned things to him like the fact that you might not be as bright as he thought you were or something like this, he always accused us of being too modest. My father wasn't a cold person. He was fairly warm but I can never remember him as the type of person that I would ever go to with a problem and discuss it with him. I think in a way he always looked down on people that were kind of pals to their children. He always used to comment that children had all the pals they needed but they needed a father and he was a father to his children. I can't remember any real problems he had.

Subject 2. My father – he's head of a section in a manufacturing corporation. He's interested in sports. Since he's become a Protestant he's a very good Protestant. Oh, he and I – we get along pretty well. I love him a lot but I get exasperated at him at times. I lived with him while my husband was overseas for six months and finally I left because he told me that if I couldn't raise my children the way he wanted them raised I could leave. I said. 'Well, I'll leave then.'

Subject 3. My father is a kindly person, strong-headed; I always felt that I shouldn't contradict him. It either made him – well, he seemed to be quite angry if he was argued with. He is a bus-driver, that's how he earned our keep most of the years we were growing up . . . And he's a strong believer in being honest and loyal to your country. He's a very patriotic person. Honesty was encouraged in our home and he was very honest with his children and I always remember admiring him and I found it very easy to talk with him on almost any problem as I grew up in my teenage years, and problems with fellows and dates and necking and kissing – I could talk to him about very freely. I could tell I could go to him with any of the problems, and religion plays a very strong part in his life and my life because of my parents. And he was always interested and busy in civic affairs and is on the school board . . . I think he finds it difficult to be effective by giving people work. It's easier for him to do it himself than to give it or to trust others with it.

Subject 4. My father was . . . a very loving man and he had a pretty tough childhood, as I can understand, although he's never said it outright . . . My dad has many interests but most of them are involved in the outdoors. He loves to fish and loves to hunt. He's the type of person who could be perfectly happy in a one-room shack in the middle of a forest . . . because he's a real true woodsman. His work – he works in an automobile factory. He's been doing this for a number of years . . . His beliefs: he's quite a devoted Christian, I feel. Politically he's definitely a conservative, not an extremist. His problems: my dad's the sort of guy who doesn't look like he's got any problems but I'm sure he does and I never realized this about him until I was quite grown. But he appears to be a very happy person and he enjoys life and he enjoys people. And concerning his relationship with me, I guess I almost feel as if he has a better relationship with me than he does with my two brothers. I was his only daughter, his pride and joy. He sang to me, he rocked me, he played with me. He did all kinds of things.

Subject 5. My father . . . was not born in this country. He has ideas which stem from more of a Victorian upbringing, strictness and moral dictates. He's interested in very serious subjects. He's a doctor. He likes nature; he likes to garden; he likes animals; I guess I acquired my interest in these things from being around him, although we didn't do that much together. That was just communicated to me, I think, more than being involved with these things together. I don't know what his beliefs are. Primarily, I guess, in general, they are, abide by the golden rule; he has a great deal of belief in doing good to others. He doesn't like to cut corners; he doesn't like to lie or to cheat to gain any ends. He doesn't pay any attention to other people around him who are perhaps involving themselves in this kind of means to attain what they want, and this has been a problem in his work because others have advanced beyond him because he has followed this virtuous sort of a pattern. His relationship with me is practically non-existent. We didn't spend much time together when I was a child and consequently I formed ideas contrary to his as far as traditional and conventional moralities go. Because we didn't spend time together and he didn't have time to grow with me and to understand me, we don't have a relationship now. At the time when he would have spent time with me I had formed other friends and desired other companions so we were just ready at the wrong time for each other.

These excerpts particularly highlight the differences between the high- and low-orgasmic women in the degree to which they recall the father as having been absent (either actually or psychologically because of incapacitating symptoms like alcoholism) and characterized by clear and definite expectations with regard to how the daughter should behave.

It is remarkable that orgasm consistency was found to be completely unrelated to women's reports of how the mother treated them. One would have thought that a mother's influence on daughter would exceed the father's, the usual view is that the daughter models herself after the mother and derives her feminine identity from the way she experiences the mother. However, there are a number of new studies which call for a revision of this view.

It is beginning to look as if the father has great importance in the sex typing of his daughter. He seems to be the agent who is most concerned about whether the children conform to sex-role expectations. One observer notes (Bronfenbrenner, 1961, p. 249):

> ... generally speaking, it is the father who is especially likely to treat children of the two sexes differently – girls receive more affection, attention and praise than boys – especially from their fathers.

There are now many studies which report closer correlations between daughter and father qualities than between those of daughter and mother. For example, one study (Fish, 1969) found that the most feminine girl was one who had had plenty of opportunity to interact with her father. It is, in fact, true that the father provides a girl with her first imporant relationship with a man. It is from her contacts with him that she gets her notions about maleness and the nature of heterosexual ties. So, the fact that orgasm consistency was found to be correlated with the woman's recall of her father's behaviour but not her mother's may not be as paradoxical as it first appears.

Voice Quality

Let me briefly describe one other positive finding which is rather intriguing, but whose implications are not yet clear. While reviewing a series of tape recordings in which high- and low-orgasmic women described themselves, I became aware of an apparent difference in the voice quality of the two groups. The high orgasmic seemed to be characterized by a greater range of tones and by a greater flexibility in the way they used their voices. They seemed to introduce more variations in their voice style by use of emphasis, prolonging words, sighs, and perceptible expiration or inspiration of breath as a dramatic counterpart to their words. To put it in another way, the low-orgasmic woman's voice seemed to be overcontrolled, narrow, and somehow mechanical in quality. To determine whether my impressions were valid, a study was undertaken in which judges were asked to blindly evaluate taped excerpts of high- and low-orgasm women. It was found that they could meaningfully distinguish the two kinds of voices. They particularly perceived the high orgasm voices as less constricted, more natural, and more often using emphatic or dramatizing sounds like sighs and deep breaths. How can we relate this difference in voice quality to the other findings already described which highlight the importance of fear of loss of love objects in the whole process of orgasm inhibition? A speculative possibility that comes to mind is that a woman who, as a child, doubted the permanence of the important figures in her world might be fearful of 'opening up' in her emotional involvements with them. That is, she might restrict her emotional commitments and expressions to a narrow, rather superficial band because she was frightened of the ultimate disappointment that would result from a deeper involvement. Presumably, her guarded attitude would be finally echoed in her constricted, artificial, non-varying voice style. But, of course, this is only speculation.

Orgasmic capacity proved to be positively involved with several other variables, but they are of a rather complicated and technical character. For example, high- and low-orgasmic women differ in the way they perceive things in the space to the right versus left of themselves. They also differ in how they experience tickle sensations on the right versus left sides of the body. There was, too, an interesting trend for the low-orgasmic women to be especially sensitive in detecting touch applied to the skin. A detailed review and interpretation of these findings appears in *The Female Orgasm.*

Comments

The central communication of the positive findings has been that the prime difference between women who are high and low in orgasmic consistency concerns their alarm about losing what they love. The low-orgasmic woman, as contrasted to the high-orgasmic, feels that persons she values and loves are not dependable, that they may unpredictably leave her. She seems to be chronically preoccupied with the possibility of being separated from those with whom she has intimate relationships.

This preoccupation actually represents what is only an exaggerated version of a type of fear which particularly characterizes women in Western culture. Many studies have shown that fears of being rejected and losing love are relatively more common in women than in men.

Manosevitz and Lanyon (1965) reported that in their questionnaire study concerned with the fears of women and men, women obtained their highest score in responding to a question about 'being rejected by others'. Of twelve questions that evoked the greatest admission of fear from the women, seven pertained to interpersonal issues. Gleser, Gottschalk, and Springer (1961) analysed five-minute samples of spontaneous speech of male and female psychiatric patients and demonstrated that concern with fears about being separated from others was significantly higher in the females than the males. Bradford (1968) devised a reliable scoring system for evaluating anxiety about loss of love, as expressed in imaginative stories, and affirmed the hypothesis that women would manifest more such anxiety than men. In discussing the possible origin of 'loss of love' anxiety in women, Bradford conjectures (p. 88):

> It might be argued that from infancy on, females are encouraged to be people and home oriented; that parents tend to use withdrawal of love rather than physical punishment in disciplining girls and thus their extreme sensitivity to this threat...

Lewis (1969) exposed females and males to a film containing a loss-of-love theme and found that the former were made more anxious by it than were the latter.

Lowery (1965) has even found that the woman's concept of death conforms to her special investment in interpersonal contact and avoiding loss of love. He concluded on the basis of an empirical analysis of imaginative productions that (p. 183): '... females tend to see death as a force which threatens to rob them of love or ... to put them out of communion with the objects of their love.' By way of contrast, he noted that males tend to see death as a form of failure or mutilation ('castration').

How does concern about loss of objects get translated into diminished orgasm consistency? There are really a number of explanatory models that one might consider, some more fanciful than others. The simplest possibility would revolve about the concept of generalized anxiety. One could merely assume that chronic concern about loss of objects is disturbing and leads to a general build-up of anxiety which ultimately interferes with the physiological processes involved in attaining orgasm. After all, it is a well-documented fact that anxiety can disrupt many kinds of physiological and motoric sequences. However, the simple anxiety model is not very tenable because it has been shown that high- and low-orgasmic women do not differ in their *overall* levels of anxiety, as measured by a variety of techniques.

One could quite fancifully speculate that since intercourse is an act which is usually seen as having obvious life-creative functions, it is particularly disturbing to those who have conflicts related to death and object loss, which represent the opposite pole of creation. That is, an act which denotes creation of new life could, in terms of its antithetical meaning, activate and reinforce anxieties which involve concern about the death or loss of important objects. The low-orgasm capacity of the woman with concern about loss (death) would derive, then, from the fact that each time she engaged in intercourse the meaning of the act (with reference to the creation-death concept) would arouse a special, focal species of anxiety which would interfere with what would otherwise be a 'natural' sequence of arousal. This model does not make any assumptions about differences in *general* levels of anxiety between the low- and high-orgasmic, but only with regard to differences in anxiety aroused by an act with a specific kind of meaning. Presumably, only stimuli which stirred feelings pertaining to creation-death (or loss) would evoke a differential quantity of anxiety in high- as compared to low-orgasmic women.

A third model to consider derives directly from psychoanalytic theory. Freud proposed that separation anxiety (fear of object loss) represents at one level a fear of nonsatisfaction, a sense of danger about the *build-up* of tension from a need which remains unsatisfied because of the absence of an important person (for example, mother) who previously took responsibility for it. More specifically, he suggested that when a child loses an important figure for any length of time he begins to build up intense, almost intolerable internal tensions as the result of unfulfilled needs which are suddenly no longer cared for; and he learns to equate such intolerable body tensions with the concept of object loss. Object loss becomes identified with the danger of being overwhelmed by an excess of body excitation stemming from unsatisfied wants. If one were to accept Freud's formulation concerning the nature of this anxiety about loss, it would provide a fairly logical sounding framework for interpreting the findings of the present studies concerning the link between fear of loss of object and orgasmic difficulties. Since the low-orgasmic women were found to be concerned about object loss (separation anxiety) one could say that, in Freud's terms, they were really fearful of an uncontrollable accumulation of internal tension (such as presumably arises from needs that are not properly cared for). One is then confronted with the obvious fact that the attainment of orgasm is a process which involves, for most persons, a uniquely enormous build-up of tension or excitation. There are probably few life experiences which set in motion such a dramatic upsurge of excitation in the normal individual. Putting these observations together, one could theorize that the woman who fears object loss has difficulty attaining orgasm because the thing she most specifically fears is the type of accumulation of tension which is basic to becoming sexually aroused. Presumably, the very act of becoming charged with excitation would, at some level, be interpreted as a reinstatement of a feeling state which signifies losing important love objects. This would, indeed, be an attractive theory if there were some supportive empirical evidence for Freud's equation of separation anxiety and fear of being overwhelmed by unsatisfied body tensions.

Of course, still another possible approach to the findings of the present study would be within the already elaborated framework which underscores the symbolic death implications to the individual of the blurring (and even loss) of consciousness that occurs during orgasm. There is good evidence that the state of consciousness is affected by a build-up of sexual excitation and that there may even be momentary lapses of reality contact during orgasm (Kinsey, *et al.*, 1953; Masters and Johnson, 1966). Psychoanalytic theorists (particularly Keiser, 1952) and also others have suggested that unconsciously the individual may experience an analogy between such blurring of consciousness and dying. There are actually descriptions in the clinical literature of persons who seemed to be frightened by orgasm because of its death implications. If it were true that orgasm has death connotations, one could understand why the woman whose ink-blot responses are characterized by an unusual amount of concern about death imagery and who in other ways is preoccupied with the potential loss that death (or other forms of separation) can bring, would find orgasm threatening and actually want to avoid it.

Although this explanatory framework emphasizes the role of fading consciousness and the need to withdraw attention from outside objects as major elements in interfering with orgasm attainment in the woman with separation anxiety, it does not rule out the impact of other factors mentioned earlier. For example, it could well be true that the creative significance of the act of intercourse, via its associated antithetical meanings, does conjure up the theme of death (that is, the continuum of creation-death) and therefore is disturbing to the woman with separation anxiety who is concerned about death as a representation of loss. Similarly, it could well be true, as Freud theorized, that separation anxiety is primarily a fear of an uncontrollable accumulation of internal tension (presumably associated with the loss of an important figure whose task it was to satisfy the need producing the tension); and so one of the factors which might inhibit orgasm in the woman with separation anxiety would be her desire to avoid the kind of build-up in body tension that mean danger to her.

What is central to the formulation that has been offered here is the idea that orgasm difficulty in women is fundamentally a function of anxiety about the lack of permanence of love objects. The conditions that might feed into such anxiety could range widely. Any feelings or fantasies created by the nature of the intercourse situation which somehow intensify anxiety about loss and related themes like death could contribute to inhibiting sexual responsiveness in the woman who is already concerned about such themes.

It is important to assert that the woman who is concerned about object loss does not represent a particular personality type. As shown by the research presented in this chapter, she is not characterized by any one trait or specific cluster of traits. There are probably innumerable ways in which a woman could adapt to anxiety about loss. She could be very careful and guarded about how she set up relationships with others; but also she might cope with her concern by compensatorily being very outgoing and seeking to cement every possible contact. She might just as equally be dependent or independent, friendly or aggressive, and so forth. Similarly, one would have to say that just because a woman has anxiety about loss of objects does not mean that she is weaker or more maladjusted or more neurotic than the average woman. There is no one problem or conflict which has been shown to predominate among those who are most psychologically distressed. It is likely that most women with anxiety about object loss develop adequate defences for coping with it. They probably learn to cope with such anxiety and to keep its influence from intruding significantly into most situations. One may theorize that only in very specialized contexts where there is a dramatic loss of investment in outside objects or in which fantasies about death are mobilized does the anxiety about object loss seriously intrude into a woman's ability to function adequately.

5. *Vaginal-Clitoral Preferences*

Aside from the matter of what facilitates or inhibits orgasm in women, the next most prominently discussed issue concerns the relative contributions made by vaginal and clitoral stimulation to orgasm attainment. Questions have been raised as to the real nature of the differences between so-called 'vaginal' and 'clitoral' stimulation. The psychoanalytic view has been that 'clitoral' and 'vaginal' orgasms are of a basically different character and represent different levels of 'psychosexual maturity'. Presumably, the vaginally produced orgasm occurs only in the woman who has mastered important major conflicts and achieved a well-integrated female identity. The woman who can reach orgasm only through clitoral stimulation is said to be immature and not to have resolved fundamental conflicts about sexual impulses. Kinsey, *et al.* (1953) and Masters and Johnson (1966) have questioned this formulation. They consider that their data demonstrate little responsiveness to stimulation of the vagina, as such; and they attribute a large part of sexual arousal in the female to direct or indirect stimulation of the clitoris. They indicate that clitoral stimulation may occur as a result of direct manual or oral manipulation by the male or indirectly as a function of the penis or the male symphysis pressing upon structures (for example, labia minora) which in turn mechanically affect the clitoris. We attempted in the present studies to find out more about the role of clitoral and vaginal stimulation. The women in all samples were asked to indicate their perception of how much clitoral as compared to vaginal stimulation contributes to their reaching orgasm. They expressed their judgements on a seven-point scale which at one extreme asserted that the major contribution was from direct clitoral stimulation and at the other extreme that the major contribution was from stimulation of the vagina. The actual question to which they responded was as follows:

This question concerns the relative importance of clitoral as compared to vaginal stimulation in your attaining orgasm. Put a circle around the appropriate number.

1. Clitoral stimulation contributes much more than vaginal stimulation.
2. Clitoral stimulation contributes somewhat more than vaginal stimulation.
3. Clitoral stimulation contributes a little more than vaginal stimulation.
4. Vaginal stimulation and clitoral stimulation make an equal contribution.
5. Vaginal stimulation contributes a little more than clitoral stimulation.
6. Vaginal stimulation contributes somewhat more than clitoral stimulation.
7. Vaginal stimulation contributes much more than clitoral stimulation.

The average response fell halfway between the category 'I prefer a moderate amount of clitoral stimulation' and the category 'I prefer a considerable amount of clitoral stimulation.' The average woman in the range of samples studied attaches more importance to clitoral than to vaginal stimulation. The difference, while not apparently great, is consistent. Actually, analysis of the percentage of women endorsing the various specific clitoral-versus-vaginal judgement categories suggests that the difference may be even greater than the comparison of averages indicates. About 29 per cent of the women across the various samples studied indicated that 'clitoral stimulation contributes much more than vaginal stimulation' to attaining orgasm. Another 20 per cent endorsed the statement that 'clitoral stimulation contributes somewhat more than vaginal stimulation'. Contrastingly, approximately 7 per cent across samples endorsed the statement that 'Vaginal stimulation contributes much more than clitoral stimulation'; and only another approximately 5 per cent indicated that 'Vaginal stimulation contributes somewhat more than clitoral stimulation.' Overall, one can see that about 49 per cent of the women assigned high importance to clitoral stimulation in achieving orgasm, while only about 12 per cent attributed equally high importance to vaginal stimulation.

Detailed analysis of the replies to the question concerning the relative importance of clitoral versus vaginal stimulation in attaining orgasm also highlighted the relatively greater arousal potency ascribed to clitoral stimulation. Roughly 19 per cent of the women indicated, 'I cannot attain orgasm without clitoral stimulation.' Another roughly 35 per cent stated that they prefer a 'considerable amount' of clitoral stimulation in the process of attaining orgasm. Only about 3 per cent across the six samples said that they do 'not prefer' any clitoral stimulation when trying to achieve orgasm.

With regard to this same issue, the women in one sample were asked to respond to the following question: 'If you had the choice of receiving only clitoral or only vaginal stimulation, which would you select?' 64 per cent stated they would choose clitoral stimulation, while 36 per cent gave their vote to vaginal.

To further clarify how women feel about clitoral versus vaginal stimulation, two samples were asked to respond to the following instruction:

> Describe as best you can the differences between vaginal and clitoral stimulation. Enumerate any differences in body sensation, intensity, mood, and so forth that you can recall.

Here are some representative excerpts from those who wrote descriptions which emphasized the special importance of clitoral stimulation in attaining orgasm.

> With vaginal stimulation I have a rather cool sweat all over my body. It is a very long and lingering feeling. There is no great intensity, only consistency of the mood and feeling. It can even become a sleeping feeling with no desire to continue. Clitoral is much more dramatic and intense. It is a hot, sweating feeling all over. It is more demanding and brings forth much better results.

> This has changed since having my baby. I enjoyed vaginal as well as clitoral stimulation before being pregnant; . . . and now enjoy clitoral stimulation exclusively and find vaginal stimulation very uncomfortable. Clitoral stimulation, on the other hand, makes me

feel very warm all over, very relaxed and at the same time eager, and is a very intense sensation.

Clitoral stimulation is more exciting because it tingles and makes the whole vaginal area pulsate. My body feels warm all over and as it is continued the intensity grows. Vaginal stimulation feels good but it can't make me achieve orgasm.

Vaginal stimulation works slower for me than clitoral stimulation. Clitoral stimulation tends to build the excitement faster and the orgasm is more intense. I feel I can grip the penis better. Vaginal stimulation is slower, so this can also be enjoyable if the need is not intense.

Clitoral stimulation is much more stimulating. There is hardly any sensation with vaginal stimulation. The (clitoral) feeling is highly intense. Sometimes it feels *too* good. Vaginal stimulation is much more sobering. It feels good but not in the same kind of way.

Vaginal stimulation is not as intense as clitoral stimulation. It is slower and less exciting. It seems only to affect that one part of my body, while clitoral stimulation makes almost my whole body react and is much more exciting and quicker.

Note the following representative comments from women in the group who obviously preferred vaginal over clitoral stimulation.

Vaginal stimulation is a more intense feeling and throbbing and an orgasm is reached faster with this, whereas clitoral stimulation is usually done in the beginning and the sensations are not as intense.

Clitoral stimulation can be felt more sharply. It is a tickling, uncomfortable feeling. Vaginal stimulation is more pleasing, more comfortable, less intense.

Vaginal stimulation is more deep and satisfying. Clitoral stimulation takes much longer to reach an equal amount of excitement. Vaginal stimulation causes faster orgasm and is definitely much more intense.

Vaginal stimulation is much more stimulating to me. It makes me excited rapidly, makes me feel ecstatic, like I can't control myself. Clitoral stimulation makes me feel good but doesn't excite as fast or as intensely as vaginal stimulation.

Vaginal stimulation is more gratifying than clitoral stimulation because it gives me a more whole and complete feeling. It is a deeper feeling than clitoral stimulation and I respond better. Clitoral stimulation does tend to aggravate me after a while.

Note the comments of several women who feel that they obtain important gratification from both clitoral and vaginal stimulation.

Clitoral stimulation is a more acute sensation; vaginal is somehow broader and vaguer though it may be just as exciting if I am desirous and ready for it. Clitoral stimulation can excite me at a much earlier phase of love-making than can vaginal. Clitoral can completely physically satisfy me, as it does when I masturbate, but emotionally the vaginal is often necessary since it (intercourse) makes me feel closer to my husband. Vaginal stimulation before intercourse does not usually excite me, although it has sometimes.

Clitoral stimulation has a high intensity – feelings concentrated in one spot. It's a lightness, a spark, almost ticklish sensation. I feel sort of an electricity. I feel the pleasure is all physical. In a vaginal stimulation the pleasure is mental or spiritual, a feeling of depth or meaning. A wider area of pleasurable sensation. It produces a longing or hunger. It is a comforting pleasure. Vaginal stimulation is like a warm bath of pleasure while clitoral is a spark of pleasure. My whole body responds to vaginal stimulation; and it moves and it feels. In clitoral stimulation my body is rigid with expectation of continuing pleasure. Vaginal stimulation is like a hum but clitoral is a high pitched note. From clitoral stimulation my body demands to be satisfied, from vaginal my body is content even if it's not.

Clitoral stimulation seems to set off a reaction of feeling that shoots straight up through my entire body through the core of me. Vaginal stimulation feels like I am being filled up – not so much an exciting feeling as clitoral stimulation. Clitoral stimulation sends chills up and down me whereas vaginal stimulation is more of an emotional feeling, rather than a physical one. Clitoral stimulation is a much more intense feeling; presents a feeling of urgency more than vaginal stimulation.

Before sexual intercourse I am stimulated greatly by foreplay involving the clitoris. And even during intercourse, especially right after entry, I am very stimulated by strokes closer to the clitoris and direct stimulation. Right before orgasm, however, I enjoy deeper penetration and more vaginal stimulation. Vaginal stimulation at the very beginning of intercourse is not as pleasurable to me as it is right before orgasm.

Vaginal – full, warm, deep feeling. Can be prolonged. Clitoral – sharp, intense, almost uncomfortably pleasurable. Not enhanced by prolonging (like tickling), but by repetition.

Clitoral stimulation is more intensive and produces a more violent reaction . . . Vaginal stimulation is much more relaxing and much less intense. I *like* it. I *love* clitoral stimulation . . . vaginal stimulation is soothing and produces a rhythmical rocking and rotating of the pelvis . . . It is never intense as clitoral stimulation, yet feels extremely good in its own way. The best analogy I can contrive is the difference between someone lightly and caressingly stroking your bare back or arm or face and being violently, exhaustingly tickled. The former resembles vaginal, the latter clitoral stimulation. Vaginal stimulation soothes me and produces an involuntary contented hum deep in my throat. The vaginal stimulation of intercourse produces a closeness, a coordination, a sense of *oneness* unmatched by any other sexual activity.

Impressionistically scanning the comments the women offered, I was struck by how often clitoral stimulation is described with words like 'warm', 'ticklish', 'electrical', and 'sharp', whereas vaginal stimulation is more often referred to as 'throbbing', 'deep', 'soothing' and 'comfortable'. It is difficult to encompass such differences with a simple generalization; and it would be premature to do so without further studies. Interestingly, there were no differences between the clitoral and vaginally oriented with respect to the degree to which their excitement was felt to involve local or restricted body areas versus the body as a whole. It is also noteworthy that those who are apparently either clitorally or vaginally oriented may find the nonpreferred form of stimulation to be actually painful or uncomfortable. There were several women who so described the effects of the nonpreferred stimulation.

In any case, the material just cited above indicates clearly that women do differ considerably in their reactions to stimulation applied manually to the clitoris and that experienced when the penis is inserted into the vagina. There may be strong preferences for one or the other but the overall trend is for clitoral to be experienced as contributing more to orgasm achievement than does vaginal.

Since Kinsey, *et al.* (1953) and Masters and Johnson (1966) cite evidence that the vagina has few sensory receptors and that penile stimulation does, in fact, indirectly produce a good deal of clitoral arousal, one is left a bit puzzled about why there should be different feeling states associated with clitoral versus vaginal modes of stimulation. I would speculate that each of the two forms of stimulation does, in terms of its specific approach, evoke arousal in a somewhat special way. The vaginal form of stimulation may arouse more intense kinesthetic sensations; may more obviously represent being penetrated and holding a friendly object within one's body; may conform more to the conventional image of 'sexual union'; and may have more 'comforting' connotations. If it is true that so-called vaginal arousal is (from a physiological perspective) primarily a form of clitoral arousal, the fact remains that it represents an approach that has unique psychological connotations (perhaps because the culture has so long had notions about there being such a uniqueness). The written comments of many of the women concerning their experiences during vaginal intercourse leave little doubt that they perceive it and 'feel' it as more than just a variant on clitoral arousal.

Relationship of Vaginal-Clitoral Preferences to Other Aspects of Sexual Behaviour

The information derived by asking each woman to rate the degree to which she prefers vaginal as compared to clitoral stimulation was compared to other aspects of her sexual behaviour. It was found that clitoral-vaginal preference was largely unrelated to most of these other aspects. Illustratively, it is not correlated with a woman's orgasm consistency, preferred or actual intercourse frequencies, self-rating of sexual responsiveness, strength of orgasm, number of intercourse positions used per month, length of foreplay, and so forth. It should be added that clitoral-vaginal preference is also not correlated with age, number of children, number of years of marriage, age of onset of menses, and other developmental indices. However, beginning with the very first study undertaken, an interesting trend appeared with regard to the correlation of clitoral-vaginal preference with the quality of the orgasm experience. One of the things that each woman was requested to do was to describe the qualitative feelings she experienced during orgasm. This was done by showing her a list of ten phrases ('strange', 'ecstatic', 'slightly embarrassed', 'happy', 'tense', 'weak', 'tired', 'unsatisfied', 'as if I would burst', 'not like myself') and asking her to rank them in terms of how well they depict her experience during orgasm. One of the terms which the women ranked in describing their experience during orgasm showed consistencies in its correlations with the clitoral-vaginal index. There was a significant trend such that the greater a woman's clitoral preference, the more likely she was to experience orgasm as having an ecstatic quality. That is, the woman with clitoral preference emphasizes the ecstatic nature of the orgasm experience; the woman with vaginal preference is less likely to do so. This difference hints at what will be presented as one of the major psychological differences between those who have vaginal versus clitoral preferences. In dictionary terms, ecstatic means 'being in a state beyond all reason and self-control, as when obsessed by a powerful emotion.' In other words, the woman with the clitoral orientation exceeds the woman with the vaginal orientation in 'feeling' orgasm in a powerful, overwhelmingly exciting fashion. The vaginal orgasm might be said to be more muted or dampened in its impact. This finding which portrayed the vaginally oriented woman as experiencing her arousal in a relatively more muted fashion took on interesting significance when viewed in the context of findings concerning the greater prevalence of feelings of body depersonalization in the vaginal as compared to the clitoral oriented.

Depersonalization

Among the things considered about each woman was her attitude towards her own body. After all, body feelings and sensations are at the core of sexual excitement. Numerous dimensions of the woman's body images were evaluated. One, called Depersonalization, turned out to be of special importance with respect to vaginal-clitoral preference. It concerns the extent to which an individual perceives her body as alien or foreign, lacking sensory vividness. A standardized questionnaire (Fisher, 1970) was used to determine the amount of Depersonalization. In order to obtain a high score for this dimension a woman had to agree with such statements as the following:

My body feels like a non-living object
My hands feel like they are not mine
My body feels 'dead'
I feel distant from my own body
I seem less aware of my body
My body is less sensitive than it usually is

Depersonalization reflects a perception of your body as lacking vitality or arousal or 'alive' quality. It was found that the more a woman describes her body as 'depersonalized', the more she prefers vaginal rather than clitoral stimulation. This finding impressed me as having an intriguing congruence with the fact that the woman with high vaginal preference was inclined to describe her orgasm as lacking 'ecstatic' quality. Just as the high vaginal woman apparently experiences the body state called orgasm in a non-ecstatic fashion, she also refers to her body as lacking experiential intensity in a more general characteristic fashion. This raised the question whether the more vaginally oriented woman might have a need to dampen or decrease the intensity of her body experiences. Her perception of orgasm as lacking 'ecstatic' quality might be regarded as one side of a broader adjustment strategy. In fact, the possibility presented itself that it might be an expression of an even more pervasive inclination to dampen sensory input from one's environment.

Awareness of Foetus

Findings obtained from one sample of women who were pregnant provided an opportunity to test in a unique way the relationship between degree of vaginal preference and the tendency to depersonalize or mute body experience. Each woman in this sample was asked to rate on a five-point scale the frequency with which she thought about the foetus inside of her body. The developing foetus represents a new major source of body experience to the pregnant woman. If the formulation presented above concerning the muting of body experience is valid, one would expect that the greater a woman's vaginal orientation, the less often she would think about the foetus. That is, she would mute or depersonalize it as an experiential source. This view was tested by correlating the clitoral-vaginal index with the frequency with which each woman indicated she thought about the foetus. The two measures proved to be significantly correlated in the predicted direction. It was indeed true that the greater a woman's vaginal preference the more likely she was to mute her awareness of the foetus within her body.

Muting of The World

As already mentioned, the fact that the more vaginally oriented woman perceives her body as depersonalized or muted in its intensity raises the question whether she might also experience other (non-body) aspects of the world in an analogously muted fashion. Could her subdued mode of 'feeling' her body be part of a general inclination to minimize the intensity of the experienced world – to reduce input from it? One of the major ways in which this possibility was explored was to compare the imaginative story productions of high-clitoral-preference women with those of high-vaginal-preference women. The question was whether the two sets of stories could be distinguished on the basis of how excitement and tension are handled. It was found that this could be done. Judges who were asked to read stories from high vaginal and high clitoral women (without knowing which women had written which stories) were able to distinguish them in terms of whether tension was glossed over or denied. The stories of the vaginally oriented were typified by the following:

No one in the story experiences a difficulty or problem. Emphasis is placed upon how happy and satisfied the story characters are. When a problem or difficulty is mentioned, it is explicitly dismissed as minor.

There is a 'they lived happily ever after' type of ending to the story. This distinction was reliably demonstrated in several groups of stories.

The difference in character between the vaginal and clitoral perspectives can be made more concrete by quoting some representative stories given by each group in response to the same picture. First, note the following examples from the vaginal extreme:

Example 1. It is a fall evening and this woman has completed her day's activities and has the children tucked soundly in bed. The weather is quite warm and she is tired. They live on a farm and have worked hard physically all day. The husband left right after the evening meal to do some church work and as the children are asleep and the last of the dishes put away, this woman sinks into a chair reminiscing over the day's activities and awaiting the return of her husband so they might spend a few moments together before retiring to bed.

Example 2. The young woman is portrayed as pensive. Her thoughts are of another day, another time, another place. Her memories take her to the small town where she spent her early years. The simplicity of that life seems far away now – and far beyond her reach. The sad realization has come to her that the only reality lies in the quiet of the ocean shore and the wind in the trees.

Example 3. A woman sitting, looking very pensive. She is an older woman, not a girl. I would surmise that she is sitting there at the end of the day, thinking over the day's activities. She doesn't look sad or happy – she looks content. She looks as though she feels tired because of a busy day with hard but satisfying work.

The themes are about as subdued as one can imagine. Now, scan some examples from the clitoral extreme.

Example 1. Mrs X is sitting waiting for her labourer husband to come home from work. They live in a semi-rundown tenement in a large city. Mrs X is quite different in looks and temperament than her husband. Possibly she is from the country and not used to the brutalization of emotions and compassion which occurs in the city. She may never accustom herself to it either.

Example 2. This is a young woman who is living around 1850. She is a farmer's wife on one of our desolate western plains. This morning her husband went to the only town to sell their crop. It has been a bad year and without a good price they are going to have to admit defeat and go back east. It is late now, after 8.00 p.m. He should have been back before 6.00 p.m. She is waiting and wondering. Their whole future depends on the news he brings home. She is impatient to know but is still a little reluctant to learn if it is bad news. She wonders over and over her life with her husband and wonders what the future will be like.

Example 3. A woman is sitting backwards on a chair – deep in thought. She has been doing some cleaning in her home; has on old clothes and has paused a moment in her work to think. She is thinking about her husband who has taken a trip and about her children who are in school. She thinks about what the future holds for her. Should she think about a career outside her family - and what is her major area of interest? She thinks about what her husband is doing and hopes that he will return soon. She thinks about how quickly her children are growing. In a few years they will be finished with school and she will be bored sitting at home all day long.

Here one sees persistent nonresolution of tension; there is no quiescence.

Anxiety

Another difference between the high-vaginal and high-clitoral-preference woman that was discovered concerns level of anxiety. Many different techniques were used to evaluate the amount of anxiety typifying each woman. Laboratory personnel who had the opportunity to observe her for extended periods, sometimes under trying circumstances, rated how anxiously she behaved. Further, her anxiety was evaluated from her response to self-descriptive questionnaires, her autobiographical account of her life, the amount of troubled tension visible in her ink-blot fantasies, her self-ratings of amount of disturbance experienced during pregnancy and delivery, her degree of distress aroused by watching a film depicting the birth of a child, and her ability to learn efficiently when exposed to stressful conditions. The overall results showed rather convincingly that the high-vaginal woman is more anxious than the high-clitoral woman. It is, of course, an intriguing question as to why there should be a link between clitoral-vaginal preference and anxiety. This will be discussed shortly.

Attitude Towards Father

An interesting contrast was detected between the high-vaginal and high-clitoral women in their view of the father. A questionnaire was administered to several samples to evaluate how they recalled the father and mother having treated them as they were growing up. It turned out that the greater a woman's vaginal preference, the less she regarded her father as having shown affectionate approval of her. The high-vaginal woman responded negatively to such statements as the following:

My father compared me favourably with other children when I did well.
My father told me how proud he was of me when I was good.
My father praised me in front of my friends.

That is, she perceived her father as not having given her special attention, praise, and approval for 'good' behaviour.

No relationship was found between a woman's vaginal-clitoral preference and her attitudes toward her mother.

Negative Results

One should stress that clitoral-vaginal preference could not be reliably linked with many other measures. It was not correlated with such variables as the following: gross physical attributes (for example, height, weight, breast size); age of menarche; number of children; ages; number of years married; various personality parameters; parental attitudes towards sex; perceived behaviour of husband; and so forth.

Comments

What are the major conclusions to be drawn from the observations presented in this chapter?

Let us start with the findings concerned with anxiety. There seems to be good reason for concluding that the more a woman prefers vaginal stimulation, the greater is her level of anxiety. The strongly vaginally oriented woman is tense and has a low threshold for feeling disturbed. This was demonstrated not only in her overt behaviour but also her fantasies. As reported, the relatively high anxiety of the vaginally oriented woman was detected by multiple observers who got to know her while she was in the psychology laboratory. It was also revealed in her self-ratings of how disturbing it was to experience the stress of being delivered of a child in the hospital. Variously, too, it was revealed in her difficulty in dealing with learning tasks; in her ink-blot responses suggestive of discomfort and dysphoria; and in her autobiographical accounts of past emotional turbulence. These findings, as already mentioned, represent a reversal of what might have been expected within the framework of most current theories of female sexuality. It has been fashionable to regard a vaginal orientation as indicative of maturity and good adjustment, while assuming that a clitoral preference denotes inadequacy in personality development. Obviously, the facts, as they have emerged in the present studies, blatantly contradict existing theories. If these facts receive support from other investigators, a gross revision of such theories will be required. If anxiety is greater in those who are more vaginally oriented, the question arises as to its origin. Unfortunately, there is no solid information available to answer this question. But one can speculate that some of the 'muting' and depersonalizing strategies found to be characteristic of the vaginally oriented serve as defences against their anxiety. Their inclination to mute their experiences was primarily revealed in the imaginative stories they produced. Typically, they portrayed situations in which either there was very little tension or, if it was of substantial proportions, it was quickly reduced in a 'they lived happily ever after' fashion. These stories could, of course, be largely wishful and the vaginally oriented might actually have little ability to mute tension-producing stimuli.

There were clearer indications that the vaginally oriented react in a denying (muting) fashion towards their own body experiences. In several samples, degree of vaginal preference was positively correlated with depersonalization. The vaginally oriented perceive their own bodies as 'foreign', 'strange', and 'dead'. They concur with statements like 'I feel distant from my own body.' They disown their own bodies – denying them self quality. It is a reasonable speculation that they defensively react to their own body experiences in this fashion as a means of denying or controlling those aspects which are threatening or anxiety-provoking. Perhaps they are seeking to evade awareness that certain anxiety-producing events occurring in their own bodies really involve self.

If one scans past findings concerning the Depersonalization measure used in this study one finds that an intensified sense of body Depersonalization is most likely to occur when an individual feels that unusual things are happening to his body over which he has no control. For example, Fisher (1970) reported that Depersonalization scores were unusually high in persons while they were being hypnotized and given the suggestion that they could not control certain parts of their bodies. Fast and Fisher (1971) noted that depersonalization was elevated in persons who had been injected with epinephrine (without being aware of its identity) and felt the effects sweeping over them. Clausen (1971) similarly found Depersonalization sharply intensified in women who were asked to ingest a drug (Pentobarbital) whose nature was unknown to them. All of these instances just cited have in common the creation of a situation in which the individual cannot account for the unexpected and nonvoluntary things happening to his body – and in which there is consequently a reaction of 'This can't be my body. It feels foreign and distant from me.' In short, the individual disowns his body because it is perceived as the site of alien events. There are suggestions that this disowning process proceeds to the point where the individual loses some elements of the vividness and personalized awareness that permeate most person's body perceptions.

The vaginally oriented woman may perceive her body in a Depersonalized manner because it is so chronically the site of anxiety. Her anxious feelings about the world are probably represented at the body level by unpleasant sensations (muscle tension, stomach discomfort) which persist, are not easily explainable, and not much influenced by conscious intent. One would theorize that she feels seized or taken over by these body-anxiety sensations in the same fashion as those who develop body Depersonalization when they feel their bodies taken over by the effects of a drug or hypnotic suggestion. It may be that after the vaginally oriented woman has experienced and tried to defend herself against the unpleasant sensations of anxiety for long periods of time she begins to generalize her antipathy so that it includes any kind of extreme excitation. That is, she finds any sudden or major 'stirring up' of her body to resemble the body arousal linked with anxiety, and it calls forth defensive Depersonalization. One hint that this may be so was provided by the earlier cited findings that the greater a woman's vaginal orientation, the less she tends to describe orgasm as feeling 'ecstatic'. The vaginally oriented woman might be thought of as wanting to avoid such an extreme of body excitement as denoted by the term 'ecstatic'. 'Controlling' her sexual arousal so that it remains below ecstatic intensity prevents it from attaining a level of body excitement which is associated with anxiety.

Why should a preference for vaginal rather than clitoral stimulation be linked with such attributes as high anxiety level, desire to mute experience, and depersonalizing of one's own body? At this point, one can only enumerate some possibilities.

1. The simplest of explanations would be that vaginal sitmulation, while sufficient to produce orgasm, does not create a mass of body excitement as great as that aroused by clitoral stimulation. If so, the vaginal orientation could be regarded as part of an adjustment strategy directed at controlling anxiety by keeping all excitation below certain levels. The plausibility of this explanation would depend heavily upon whether vaginal excitation is somehow more controlled and less sweeping than clitoral excitation. While the findings of Masters and Johnson (1966), and Kinsey, *et al.* (1953) and also some of the qualitative reports obtained in the present study concerning the subjective experiences associated with vaginal-versus-clitoral stimulation hint that such may be true, it must be regarded as far from established.

2. A second possibility to consider is that the vaginally oriented woman, because of her depersonalized body orientation, requires the unique condition of the penis being inserted into her body in order to build up feelings of sexual arousal. That is, her depersonalized way of experiencing her body might make her relatively unresponsive to sexual stimulation unless it was delivered in a way that had unusually intense psychological connotations. The specific act of intercourse, with its special significance, might be necessary to break through the coldness or unresponsiveness possibly associated wtih a depersonalized set. Perhaps direct clitoral stimulation lacks the definition of a full or real sexual contact and therefore lacks the psychological intensity necessary to 'get through' a depersonalized way of interpreting body events. One might say

that feeling the penis inserted, with its connotations of unique intimacy, would be necessary for the depersonalizing woman to personalize sexual stimulation.

3. Another perspective on the possible relationship between vaginal orientation and the importance of penile insertion in achieving arousal derives from the relationship which was found between clitoral-vaginal preference and perception of father. It will be recalled that the greater a woman's vaginal preference, the *less* she tended to remember her father as having given her praise and reward for doing well or conforming to his expectations. That is, she recalled having had difficulty in eliciting a positive response from him. If it is assumed that such a relationship with father actually existed, the possibility arises that it became a prototype for her interactions with men in general. Thus, the greater a woman's vaginal preference, the less she might expect men to respond positively when she did things to please them. Is it possible that this relationship could be a causal one, with the attitude toward men influencing the degree of vaginal preference? Apropos of this, it is interesting that Greenacre (1966) proposed that a girl may have fantasies which involve (p. 149) 'hanging on to the father with an oral-vaginal babyish grasp.' She implied, as has also been theorized by others (Fenichel, 1945), that the vagina can be assigned symbolic meanings and be used to express attitudes towards men. It might be that a woman whose experiences with her father had led her to expect that men would not respond positively would need an extra amount of commitment from a man before she could relate sexually to him in a positive manner. This 'extra commitment' might symbolically require insertion of his penis into her vagina. She might need this special sign of intimacy from him to believe that he really intended to be friendly and to bestow affection upon her.

4. It is worth considering the possibility too that a woman who chronically depersonalizes her body (who feels distant from it) might have a relatively hazy concept of it, particularly those areas like the vagina which are difficult to perceive visually. If so, the act of intercourse which would suddenly articulate the vagina and give it clear spatial form would articulate the sexual potential of her body and make it possible for her to tune in on sexual stimula-

tion in a focused fashion. But merely stimulating the clitoris, without the spatial definition of the vagina caused by penile insertion, might fail to highlight the hazily perceived pelvic region sufficiently to permit focusing on the arousal in that region.

None of the explanatory possibilities just considered is completely convincing. Considerably more investigation and thought needs to be devoted to this problem.

6. *Intercourse Frequency, Masturbation, and Other Dimensions of Sexual Behaviour*

Many aspects of sexual behaviour besides those already described were appraised in the course of our investigations. Some of the results demonstrated surprising positive relationships between specific patterns of sexual response and personality and background factors. Still other results failed in surprising ways to show any correlations between certain sexual patterns and background factors often thought to be associated with them.

Intercourse Frequency

As mentioned earlier, the average woman we studied had intercourse about three to four times per week. In one sample the average was less than three and in another it was almost five. When asked how often she would *prefer* to have intercourse, the average woman stated that it was very close to her actual frequency. She did indicate that her husband preferred about one more intercourse contact per week than she preferred. However, she further indicated that she agrees to her husband's requests for intercourse 'almost always'.

What can one say about a woman's sexual attitudes and reactions on the basis of knowledge of how frequently she has intercourse? It has been pointed out that intercourse frequency is unrelated to orgasm consistency and clitoral-vaginal preference. But it should be added that there are trends for those women who engage frequently in intercourse:

To make use of a large number of different intercourse positions per month.
To have intercourse during the time of menstrual flow.
To sleep in the nude.
To actually *prefer* frequent intercourse (that is, they do not feel forced by their husbands to have intercourse more often than they would like).

Our research findings indicated also that the greater a woman's intercourse frequency the more narcissistic or self-focused she is. One line of evidence with regard to this point derives from findings concerning the amount of energy each woman devotes to self-grooming and enhancing her appearance. A questionnaire was administered to a number of our samples asking about a range of body-enhancing procedures. Here are some examples of the questions asked:

How often do you go to a hairdresser each month?
How many times per day, on the average, do you change your make-up?
How many times per month do you 'do your nails' or get a manicure?
How many times per week do you rub your entire body with creams, powder, or cologne?

There was a distinct trend for the women who most often engage in intercourse to devote a large amount of body-enhancing attention to themselves.

Some indirect support for the tenor of this finding came too from the observation that intercourse frequency is positively correlated with describing oneself as having an exhibitionistic orientation. Women with high intercourse rates were likely to express preferences for such as the following:

To be the centre of attention
To have others notice and comment upon one's appearance
To talk about personal achievements

They want people to lavish interest and admiration upon them. Just as they are the centre of their own body-grooming efforts, they look for opportunities to become the centre of focus for others.

This self-indulgent perspective was even further shown when information was obtained from each woman about how she distributes her time during an average week. It was found that the greater a woman's intercourse frequency the more time she turns to activities which will provide her with entertainment. She spends more time doing things like watching television, attending movies, going to parties, and listening to records. She prefers activities which will amuse or indulge her.

Why should a relationship exist between a woman's intercourse frequency and her degree of interest in narcissistic self-gratification? Obviously the simplest and most economical explanation would be that a narcissistic person particularly searches out experiences which will make her the focus of attention and enable her to be the recipient of stimulation that signifies admiration. Just as she enthusiastically invests energy in grooming and enhancing her body, she is drawn to situations in which others will provide her with analogous sensations. Her special enjoyment of the self-enhancing attention associated with intercourse would lead her to seek it frequently. It should be cautioned that this statement is in no way intended to mean that the prime determiner of a woman's intercourse rate is her degree of self-centredness, but only that it is *one* among a number of factors that probably play significant roles.

Masturbation

We found limited masturbatory activity reported among the samples of married women that were studied. While, as shown by Kinsey, *et al.* (1953) masturbation is widely prevalent among women, it occurs with low frequency (less than once per month) among those who are married and have regular intercourse available to them. The average woman in the samples which we studied indicated that she masturbates only 'rarely'; and thus conforms to the Kinsey, *et al.* norms. Few aspects of sexual behaviour turned out to be consistently related to either a woman's frequency of masturbation or the amount of satisfaction she reported deriving from it. The masturbation measures were not correlated with orgasm consistency, actual or preferred intercourse frequency, and the quality of the orgasmic experience. This would suggest that such masturbation as does occur is in no obvious way a compensation for lack or deficit in other areas of sexual experience. The masturbation measures were also not correlated with rate of sexual masturbation (as defined by age of menarche); sources of early sex information; and early dating frequency. Further, they were not correlated with number of years of marriage, number of children, and religious membership (for example, Catholic versus Protestant).

Interestingly, too, they were not linked with a number of direct and indirect measures of anxiety and maladjustment that were employed. That is, there is no indication that they reflect the 'mental health' of a woman. Of course, one should keep in mind that the women studied had very low masturbation rates. Only a small number seemed to attach really substantial importance to masturbation as a significant source of gratification. It would therefore be hazardous to generalize from the present study to women who do have high masturbation rates.

There were a few indices of sexual behaviour and sexual attitude which were found to be related to masturbation behaviour.

Masturbation frequency proved to be positively correlated with the following:

The degree of importance ascribed by each woman to sex in her own life
The extent to which movies and novels about sex provide enjoyment
The degree to which there is belief that sexual freedom in our culture should be increased
The amount of time spent thinking about sex
The frequency of intercourse during menstruation

No easy generalization presents itself with regard to the correlations just enumerated. One could say that there is a trend for those who indicate a positive investment in masturbation to express attitudes which favour explicit sexual freedom and open awareness (and appreciation) of that which has sexual significance.

When I began to think about the possible personality concomitants of masturbation behaviour in women, I surveyed the existing literature on the subject. There were a few empirical studies (Terman, 1938, 1951; Landis, *et al.*, 1940) that had systematically appraised the personality attributes of women differing with reference to masturbation; but the results were uniformly not promising. There were also a considerable number of theoretical and clinical publications that speculated concerning the psychological determinants of masturbation (Masters, 1967; Arlow, 1953). They presented a formidable array of assertions and theories. As I examined them, I found that certain statements recurred more than others. For example, it is often said that a very low incidence of masturbation during childhood signifies too great a repression or denial of sexual urges; and a high masturbation rate in an adult is usually interpreted as indicative of an avoidance of 'genuine' heterosexuality. Other speculative themes that are prominent in this literature concerning masturbation are as follows:

It represents a way of obtaining release of sexual tension without the necessity of forming a relationship with another person; and therefore permits avoidance of deep personal involvement.

It provides a form of sexual experience in which the individual retains control over the tempo and nature of what occurs and need not be exposed to the unexpected, messy events that can occur during intercourse.

It often arouses intense guilt because it is so disapproved by most parents and is linked early in life with being sinful; and is accompanied by unconscious fantasies that symbolically impart to it a grossly forbidden significance.

It encourages feelings of unreality by not only permitting retreat from the usual intimacy of the two person sexual transaction, but also by requiring the individual to split her identity by simultaneously playing two roles: the one who is delivering stimulation and also the one receiving it.

What impressed me as I became acquainted with this literature was the rather pervasive way in which masturbation was described as eliciting feelings of being sinful and dirty. While different mechanisms and models were offered to account for this effect, there was the repetitive observation that masturbation is associated with being unclean.

The findings obtained from psychological tests turned out to be supportive of this view. Quite a number of measures were taken of how much importance the woman attached to being orderly, clean, and neat. There was a significant trend indicating that the more a woman depicts herself as preferring a way of life which is orderly, systematic, and not messy the *less* she masturbates. This suggests that those who avoid masturbation do so, at least in part, because they see it as something which is dirty and makes them feel uncomfortably unclean. It should be added that masturbation frequency was lower in those who expressed a strong commitment to religious values than in those who had little such commitment.

Interest in masturbation and attitude toward one's mother were also found to be significantly linked in the women studied. Masturbation frequency was found to be negatively correlated with the degree to which mother was described as being moralistically oriented. But it was positively correlated with the degree to which she was described as having behaved in a neglecting, egocentric, distant, hostile, and nonloving fashion. The more a woman depicted her mother as an unfriendly and neglecting person the more she makes use of masturbation. However, there were no relationships between a woman's masturbation behaviour and her attitudes toward her father. The rather unique positive association between masturbation frequency and perceiving one's mother as unfriendly and neglecting calls to mind those theories which conceptualize masturbation in adults as an activity which provides sexual arousal without the necessity of giving oneself to another – without the need to give up any of one's independence. That is, if a woman were reared by a mother who kept pushing her away and refusing to relate to her with any warmth, might she not, on the basis of this prototype experience, feel that she could not expect mutuality in relationships with others and therefore that she should seek gratification in as *independent* a fashion as possible. Masturbation might be especially attractive to someone with such an orientation. It permits gratification in a context where one need relate only to self and can be unconcerned about the 'other'. While this may be true it should be cautioned that there is no evidence that the woman who enjoys masturbating is so distrustful of personal involvement that she cannot form the kind of intimate relationship with a man that occurs during intercourse leading to orgasm. I would only speculate that if a woman has had a history of feeling neglected by her mother she may have a special need to prove to herself periodically that she is capable of satisfying herself without the assistance of an outside agent (namely, mother). If so, the masturbation would not only be a sexual act but also a means of expressing a special kind of autonomy.

Repeated Orgasms in a Limited Period of Time

We discerned real differences among the women in the frequency with which they have more than one orgasm in a relatively brief period of time. In view of the Masters and Johnson (1966) report that women do not have the sort of refractory period of response to sexual stimulation that men do, one might expect that all women could potentially have many orgasms during a limited time span. The question arises, then, as to why there are differences in the frequency of such orgasm experiences. In the present samples there were no indications that such differences are due to age, number of years of marriage, or number of pregnancies. The negative results with respect to age and number of years of marriage are noted in order to indicate that 'multiple' orgasms are not simply a function of amount of sexual experience or practice. The negative result pertaining to number of pregnancies is mentioned in relation to Sherfey's (1966) hypothesis that the increase in pelvic vascularity resulting from pregnancy plays a significant part in potential for multiple orgasms.

Hostility

It has already been mentioned that orgasm capacity was not correlated with how hostile or aggressive a woman appeared to be. Multiple measures of anger and aggression have also failed to show consistent correlations with many other sexual behaviour indices. This is true despite the use of an exhaustive assemblage of techniques for measuring hostility which have diversely looked at a woman's own evaluation of her hostility behaviour, the ratings by observers of how aggressively she conducts herself, and the amount of hostility in her fantasies as elicited by pictures and ink blots. There is no evidence that the aggressive woman has either more or less intercourse per week than the nonaggressive one. Further, a woman's degree of hostility does not seem to play a role in her clitoral versus vaginal stimulation preferences, in her likelihood of having 'multiple' orgasms, in the liberality of her sexual standards, in her likelihood of agreeing to intercourse during her menstrual period, in her preferred modes of foreplay, in her degree of dissatisfaction after orgasm, and so forth. This is not a pattern of results which I would have intuitively predicted. For example, one might have expected the angry woman to have difficulties in experiencing sexual satisfaction or to be characterized by reduced intercourse rates. However, if one looks carefully at the few studies in the literature which have explored the relationship of hostility in women to sexual parameters, the findings have been mixed. Winokur (in Winokur, 1963) reported that when twenty married couples were asked to estimate how often they had been angry in a two-week period and also estimated their frequency of intercourse during this same period, the two classes of events had only a chance relationship. This was true despite the fact that when explicitly questioned about this issue, the individuals expressed the belief that when they are angry they are less 'sexually active'. But, to further complicate things, about half of the seventeen women who described themselves as becoming more irritable and quarrelsome premenstrually also said that they were more receptive to sexual relations at this time. That is, the irritability was accompanied by *higher* rather than lower sexual receptivity. Relatedly, one should also keep in mind that there are studies (Barclay and Haber, 1965) in which women seemed to find hostility sexually arousing. In short, previous observations do not support a simple theory about hostility either inhibiting or facilitating sexual responsiveness. It might 'feel' as if it were inhibitory, but at the same time arouse sexual fantasies. Or it might heighten sexual responsiveness, while at the same time interfering with the initial sociability needed to initiate intercourse.

Parental Attitudes Towards Sex and the Body

Inquiries were made across the various samples with regard to how a woman's sexual behaviour and responsiveness (beyond the dimension of orgasm capacity) are related to parental attitudes toward sex, menstruation, nudity, and also the parental role in sex education. These inquiries, based on each woman's memory of her parents, involved the following matters:

Parents' attitudes about their daughter's first menstruation
Which of the parents provided sexual information

How much the parents approved or disapproved of sex
How openly affectionate the parents were toward each other
Whether the parents' marriage was a happy one
Whether the parents could talk easily about sex and the body
Whether the mother considered it natural to see her daughter nude
How comfortable the parents were about touching their daughter's body

No consistent relationships could be found between any of these variables and a large array of sexual measures. There is no indication that the extent to which parents were free or liberal in their attitudes toward their daughter (as she recalls it) about sex or body contact played a part in her satisfactions from sex, in her preferences for particular forms of sexual stimulation, or even in the liberality of her sexual standards.

Influence of Critical Psychosexual Experiences

The women in all of the samples were asked to report how they felt at several – what are usually considered to be critical – times in psychosexual development. They were to rate their reactions (namely, their amount of disturbance) to their first menstruation, their first serious date, and their first intercourse. It was found that such reports of degree of disturbance did not correlate consistently with any of the sexual measures. The amount of trauma produced by such experiences as first menstruation or first intercourse did not have a detectable impact upon subsequent sexual behaviour. It will be recalled that in a previous chapter, which reviewed previous research dealing with the effects of early traumatic sexual experiences upon later orgasm capacity, no evidence could be mustered to support the notion that such experiences have a lasting impact. Of course, one can take the position that reports by women of how they felt many years earlier are likely to be inaccurate. However, even within the context of such inaccuracy one might at least expect that the differentiation between those reporting no trauma and those reporting a high amount of trauma would be meaningful. Yet, an analysis of these extreme categories also did not turn up any differences in sexual behaviour.

Modes and Conditions of Sexual Arousal

One noteworthy outcome of the studies we launched was to provide detailed information concerning several aspects of feminine sexual arousal, some of which have not been previously carefully scrutinized. A number of interesting sets of data will now be presented.

Foreplay

The first phase of sexual arousal occurs prior to onset of intercourse. This is the so-called period of 'foreplay', Kinsey, *et al.* (1953) and others have described the repertoire (for example, deep kissing) that the male uses during this period to excite a woman (and she to excite him). One of the requests made of the women in the several samples was to describe how aroused different areas of their bodies became during foreplay. They were asked to rank the following body areas in terms of their degree of response to foreplay stimulation:

Breasts
Outside lips of vulva
Inside lips of vulva
Vagina near clitoris
Clitoris
Inside vagina

Foreplay was rated as producing greatest excitement directly in the clitoris (whether due to oral or manual stimulation or both) and least excitement in the outside lips of the vulva. The remaining body areas were rated in the following sequence (proceeding from greater to lesser excitement):

Vagina near clitoris
Inside lips of vulva
Inside vagina
Breasts

It was striking how relatively constant the ratings were from sample to sample. In all samples the 'clitoris' and 'vagina near clitoris' were designated as the most excited of all areas. Also, 'outside lips of vulva' was usually designated as the least excited. Relatively low excitement was attributed to the 'inside of vagina'. The fact that high excitement is ascribed to the clitoris and low arousal to the vagina is nicely congruent with the observations of Kinsey, *et al*. (1953) and Masters and Johnson (1966) that the vagina is relatively low in its sensory arousability, with just the opposite holding true for the clitoris. The finding that more excitement is experienced in the inside than the outside lips of the vulva fits with the apparently greater emphasis placed by Masters and Johnson on the changes in the labia minora as compared to those in the labia majora during sexual stimulation.

Another aspect of foreplay which was appraised concerned the amount of time typically devoted to it. The mean times in the various samples range from approximately 11 to 16 minutes, with 12·5 being the median. Again it was striking how relatively constant the values are across samples. It is interesting to compare the foreplay time values in the present samples with those cited by Kinsey, *et al*. (1953). In the Kinsey, *et al*. sample it was found that foreplay was of 0 to 3 minutes duration for 11 per cent; 4 to 10 minutes for 36 per cent; 11 to 20 minutes for 31 per cent; and 21 minutes or more for 22 per cent; while in the present samples, the approximate corresponding values were 4, 50, 37, and 8 per cents. The most obvious difference between the two sets of values is the greater occurrence of very low (0 to 3 minutes) and very high (21 minutes or more) foreplay durations in the Kinsey, *et al*. data. About half of the women in the present samples indicated that their foreplay involved from 4 to 10 minutes. It was similarly true that a sizeable per cent of the Kinsey, *et al*. sample fell into this category. As noted by Kinsey, *et al*., the effort devoted by married couples to foreplay is generally brief and perfunctory. In addition, they could find no relationship between length of foreplay and probability of attaining orgasm in the female.

Sexual Excitement

One approach in the present study to analysing the experiential aspect of orgasm was to ask for ratings of the manner in which sexual excitement builds up and dissipates. Each woman was asked to rate her orgasm experience on a five-point scale ranging from, 'The excitement rises and then dies gradually' to 'Excitement reaches such a high level that release is accompanied by collapse (possibly a faint).' The average in the samples that completed this rating was closest to the second of the five categories (namely, 'Excitement mounts to a high tension followed by sudden release'). Examination of the percentages of women endorsing each of the five rating categories is informative. Only about 1–2 per cent indicated that they experience orgasm with the extreme intensity of the excitement defined by the phrase 'accompanied by collapse'; but about 5 per cent did rather consistently endorse the fourth rating alternative ('excitement increases to a point where release is accompanied by spasms or convulsions').

To ascertain whether conscious ideation or fantasy is very prominent during orgasm, the women in several samples were asked to respond to a four-point scale ranging from, 'During orgasm my mind is a complete blank' to 'During orgasm I almost always have images and pictures in my mind.' The average judgement was that 'images and pictures' only occur 'occasionally'. They do *not* seem to be a *regular* accompaniment of the orgasm experience.

Masters and Johnson (1966) observed a good deal of variation in the duration of orgasm in the women they studied. The women in several samples participating in the present study were asked to estimate the length of their orgasm. One cannot but be impressed with how relatively consistent the estimates turned out. They largely clustered within the range six to ten seconds. Apparently, as a subjective phenomenon, the typical female orgasm lasts from six to ten seconds. It is noteworthy, though, that there were a few extreme cases in the various samples in which it was reported that orgasm lasts 'more than twenty seconds'.

One of the special attempts made in the present studies to probe the feelings characterizing orgasm and also the immediate post-orgasm period involved asking the women in all of the samples to evaluate the accuracy of ten terms (for example, 'ecstatic', 'tired', 'weak', 'as if I would burst') with reference to how well they describe their feelings during orgasm and the accuracy of another ten similar terms with reference to how well they depict their feelings five minutes after orgasm.

Typically, the women in all of the seven samples thought that terms like 'ecstatic', 'happy', and 'as if I would burst' were most descriptive of how they felt during orgasm and terms like 'tense', 'slightly embarrassed', and 'unsatisfied' as least descriptive. The terms 'happy', 'relaxed', and 'satisfied' are, across all samples, most often designated as typical of the women's feelings post-orgasm and the terms 'slightly embarrassed', 'unsatisfied', and 'slightly guilty' as least typical.

Obviously, the evaluations by the women of the two sets of terms do not really reveal much about the orgasmic experience. The positive terms were consistently favoured and the negative ones not favoured. It is hardly surprising that the judgements typically portrayed the orgasm and post-orgasm experience as having favourable rather than unfavourable connotations. However, there was considerable individual variation with respect to the ranks assigned to the descriptive terms. There were women who said that feelings of being 'unsatisfied' and 'tense' were most, and feelings of 'ecstasy' least, characteristic of their orgasm experience; and similarly some depicted 'happy' and 'relaxed' as least, and 'slightly guilty' and 'unsatisfied' as most characteristic of their post-orgasm feelings.

An inquiry was made concerning how long it took women to attain orgasm from the time intercourse began and also how long they estimated their husbands usually required. The average woman who was questioned seemed to require about eight minutes to achieve orgasm, but it should be emphasized that there was amazing individual variation, with some requiring as few as one minute and others requiring as much as thirty minutes. In every sample the women estimated that it takes longer for them to attain orgasm that it does their husbands. Typically, they perceive themselves as taking from 40 to 80 per cent more time. Kinsey, *et al.* (1953) in commenting upon the relatively longer time taken by most women to attain orgasm, stated that it was not due to a lesser excitability on their part, but rather the relative inefficiency with which stimulation was applied during intercourse. They pointed out, for example, that during masturbation the average woman who could attain orgasm did so in just under four minutes.

In two of the samples the women were requested to specify the exact procedure used in attaining orgasm. They were asked to indicate which of the following alternatives best applied to them:

1. My husband stimulates me clitorally. He then inserts his penis and attains orgasm; and finally I attain orgasm after he stimulates me further clitorally.

2. My husband stimulates me clitorally until I reach orgasm and then he inserts his penis and attains orgasm himself.

3. My husband inserts his penis and attains orgasm and then stimulates me clitorally until I attain orgasm.

4. My husband stimulates me clitorally; inserts his penis and we attain orgasm at the same time.

5. If none of the above statements apply, please give a description of what is true for you.

In one sample 70 per cent indicated that they achieved orgasm via the sequence of being manually stimulated clitorally and then having their husbands insert the penis to stimulate them further, with both then attaining orgasm at approximately the same time. Twenty per cent reported that orgasm was attained by the sequence of first being manually stimulated clitorally; having the husband insert his penis and attain orgasm; and then receiving further manual clitoral stimulation which finally produced orgasm level arousal.

In another sample 55 per cent said they attained orgasm via the process of husband stimulating them clitorally and then inserting his penis and continuing intromission until orgasmic excitement was achieved in both. 45 per cent indicated that they reached orgasm via either alternatives 1, 2, or 3 listed above. All of these variants involve primarily direct clitoral stimulation to orgasm, with the husband achieving his own orgasm by intromission either before or after his wife's orgasm.

If one averages the two samples, it can be said that about 63 per cent reach orgasm by the sequence of clitoral stimulation followed by penile intromission; and about 35 per cent reach orgasm by clitoral stimulation either before or after the husband attains orgasm by intromission.

In order to get an even more precise picture of the manner in which orgasm is attained, the women in one sample were asked to answer the following questions:

What per cent of the time that you attain orgasm does it occur *at the same time* that your husband attains his orgasm?

What per cent of the time does your orgasm occur *before* your husband's orgasm?

What per cent of the time does your orgasm occur *after* your husband's orgasm?

What per cent of the time that you reach orgasm is the final stage of excitement that actually pushes you to the point of orgasm produced by your husband stimulating your clitoral area with his hand?

What per cent of the time is your husband's penis still inserted in your vagina at the moment that you actually have your orgasm?

About 35 per cent of the women indicated that they attain orgasm simultaneously with their spouses. Approximately 41 per cent said they reach orgasm before and 23 per cent after their husbands. That is, 64 per cent reach orgasm at a time other than their husbands do.

It is interesting that on the average they indicated that about thirty per cent of the time they require direct manual stimulation to give them the final push necessary to reach orgasm. 35 per cent of the women said they require such final direct manual stimulation 50 or more per cent of the time to attain orgasm. Only 20 per cent of the women said they never require a final push from manual stimulation to reach orgasm.

Finally, it was said by the women that, on the average, the husband's penis is still inserted in the vagina 57 per cent of the time that orgasm occurs. 33 per cent said the husband's penis is still inserted only 50 per cent of the time that orgasm occurs. Note also that only 33 per cent said that the husband's penis is always still inserted at the time of orgasm.

Preferred Intercourse Conditions

Interesting findings emerged when the women in one sample were asked to respond to the following instructions:

List the conditions (for example, your feelings, the physical surroundings) which seem to be most important in determining how sexually responsive you will be at any particular time that you have intercourse. Try to list at least five.

The various conditions enumerated by the women which they felt hindered or facilitated their sexual responsiveness were classified. It can be seen in the accompanying table that one of the

Percentage frequencies with which various conditions are mentioned by women as facilitating their sexual responsiveness

	Per Cent
Privacy and freedom from intrusion	18[1,2]
Good relationship between self and husband	18
Something 'good' or 'successful' occurred that day	8
Not tense or depressed	8
Not tired	8
Modulation of light (semi-darkness)	7
Not sick	6
Be clean or smell good	5
No time limit	4
Proper temperature in room	3
Occur at night	3
Previously read sexy book or seen sexy movie	3
Be somewhere unusual (motel, woods, shower)	3
Good meal previously	2
Soft music	2
Have a few drinks	2
Occur during the day	2

1. Rounded to nearest whole number.
2. Since all women mentioned multiple conditions, each per cent is equal to the total in that category divided by the total in all categories.

categories most frequently mentioned is 'privacy and freedom from intrusion'. Many of the women stressed that they could not consistently build up excitement if they were aware of persons in adjoining rooms, heard loud sounds or voices nearby, or somehow felt they were not guaranteed complete assurance against being observed by others. This finding may be regarded as especially pertinent to the fact that a number of women emphasized in their spontaneous descriptions of how they achieve orgasm, the importance of freedom from distraction and of being able to focus exclusively on their body sensations during sexual arousal. Together, these observations imply that the attainment of orgasm in a woman involves a rather unique degree of concentration upon self and a simultaneous shutting out of the outer world. The build up to orgasmic excitement seems to require an 'insulated', 'detached-from-the-world', self-absorbed state. This idea will be returned to at a later point when its implications will be discussed in relation to some of the findings bearing on the personality correlates of orgasm consistency.

When one examines the table, one finds that a number of the major conditions cited by women as helping them to be sexually responsive have to do with feeling friendly (particularly towards husband) and perceiving the world in positive rather than negative terms. Thus, 18 per cent of the citations mention 'good relationships between husband and self' and 8 per cent 'something "good" or "successful" occurring that day' as facilitating. With reference to the second of these categories, a number of women indicated that if they had achieved a valued goal or received recognition for successfully doing something in the period prior to engaging in intercourse they were particularly likely to be responsive. A good feeling about self and the world seems to be central to such facilitation. A similar sense of feeling 'good' is implied by the category 'not tense or depressed', which represents 8 per cent of the statements about conditions that enhance responsiveness. Many of the other statement categories in the table have to do with body feelings. Women say their responsiveness is greatest when they are not tired, not sick and clean – and to a lesser extent when they are experiencing an optimum room temperature and had good food, and a 'few drinks'. Scattered references are also found to the value of modulating the environment with 'soft music' and semi-darkness. A fairly low number of statements were made which concerned the value of novelty in stimulating responsiveness. Thus, three per cent of the statements referred to the value of being in a different setting like a motel room or the woods; and three per cent indicated that responsiveness was magnified if there had been previous exposure to sexual, provocative material in a book or film.

Fantasies During Intercourse

As part of the effort to obtain material concerning the nature of the intercourse experience from the women in one sample, they were requested as follows:

Please give at least two examples of thoughts or images or fantasies you have had more than once while having intercourse or during orgasm.

The following are illustrations of fantasies which were described.

Subject 1. That I was an actress in a play, experiencing one scene after another. Each position of intercourse was an act of the play, it told a part of the story. Excitement mounted as progress was made from one scene to another until the entire theme was unfolded.

Another fantasy was that I was floating over an expansive field of flowers – feeling very light and like I would never touch the ground. In a sense I felt immortal and goddess-like, very ephemeral. It was as though there was only one body, and the world consisted only of this one united body.

Subject 2. I pretend to be the greatest, most famous whore in history.

Subject 3. I fantasy that the man making love to me is not my husband, but another man – he is a man that I have an extreme physical attraction for – It occurs most when I am angry or disillusioned with my husband.

Subject 4. I used to imagine stories about girls who nursed and aided injured men who later fell in love with the girls. The first intercourse was always a glorious happening much to be desired.

Subject 5. I usually think of myself in a hospital bed, other patients on either side of me, the drapes pulled around my bed for modified privacy, my legs spread wide in stirrups, myself draped appropriately, and a doctor, faceless and nameless, examining me with a nurse nearby. Sometimes I think of my husband there, too, holding my hand.

Subject 6. I am being half forced (not really raped) by a man who may be intellectually or physically unattractive, but to whom I am nevertheless very much physically attracted to. All these men are faceless. Many times they are black men, very masculine. Sometimes they are old men and very unattractive. The idea of teasing is important.

More than 75 per cent of the women indicated that they do have at least one fantasy or image which recurs occasionally (but not frequently) during intercourse. When these fantasies were roughly categorized, it was found that about 40 per cent involved scenes in which the woman was having a sexual contact or interchange with someone other than her husband. Within this category, more than half of the instances revolved about themes in which the woman perceived herself as raped, sexually humiliated, or somehow sexually wicked. As already cited above, there were fantasies of being helplessly tied and having to submit to brutal rape; of being a cheap whore humiliated by men; of having to expose one's genitals publicly in an embarrassing way; and so forth. A number of the women fantasied that they were actresses on a stage and were performing sexually for an audience. Masochistic and exhibitionistic elements were strongly prominent in the fantasies which were collected. Another interesting category (10 per cent) fantasied the portrayed self as being a royal or superior figure (for example, goddess, princess) with special power or prestige. Illustratively, one woman said, 'I see myself like a queen in a fairy tale.'

About 30 per cent of the images reported by the women dramatized simple sensory experiences. There were references to 'red flashes', 'colours', 'water rushing', and 'things floating'. In these instances the woman would, as she engaged in intercourse, conjure up images of intense colours or swiftly flowing water or of objects and persons floating in the air. Such images seemed to be simple representations of the arousal and excitement produced by sexual stimulation.

Other less common fantasies that were mentioned may be cited to illustrate the range obtained:

A man climbing a steep mountain
A picture of husband and self combined into one person
An unknown male face
A religious ceremony
Scene from a sexy movie
Someone trying to 'castrate' me
The word 'love' on a valentine

One of the interesting aspects of the fantasy material collected is the frequency with which it concerned being with someone other than one's husband or in a different place than the immediate situation. It seemed to represent an attempt to depict self as being with a new sex partner or engaged in a novel form of sexual activity. One could think of it as a means for adding spice to an experience that has grown repetitious or stale. At another level, it might be viewed as an attempt to remove oneself from the immediate situation, a way of distancing self from what is actually occurring. It might be a way of escaping unpleasant aspects of the immediate sexual intimacy. One woman explicitly stated that while having intercourse with her husband she imagined that she was with other men because she felt so negatively towards him.

There is a noteworthy contrast between such fantasies of escape from the immediate setting and the earlier described concern that many of the women have about carefully insulating the intercourse situation against intrusion from outside.

7. Menstruation, Pregnancy, Contraception, and Their Relation to Sexuality

Considerable attention was devoted to the question of whether a woman's sexual behaviour is related in any way to her psychological adaptation to her reproductive functions. One aspect of this question would be to ask whether women differing in orgasm consistency show logically related differences in how they experience menstruation or react to the whole process of containing the growing foetus. Another would be whether a woman's mode of adaptation to her reproductive functions can be tied in any way to her personality characteristics. For example, is the woman who experiences menstruation as painful or who develops great anxiety during pregnancy less feminine than one who has no such difficulties? A considerable superstructure of theory and speculation has grown up about such issues. There is an influential, half-accepted 'scientific' folklore which thinks women are consistent in the way they deal with their sexual and reproductive capacities. It is widely accepted in some circles (for example, among psychoanalytic theorists), that a woman who is disturbed about her sex role will have menstrual difficulties and probably cope poorly with the demands of pregnancy. A woman who reports an unusual amount of menstrual pain automatically becomes suspected of having serious sexual conflicts. I had considerable opportunity in the course of studying the various samples to gather information bearing on issues of this sort. The women were asked to give detailed data concerning their menstrual patterns and there were several studies in which psychological measures were obtained on the same women during both menstrual and nonmenstrual phases. Also, one sample of women was studied during pregnancy and again a month after delivery. The menstrual and pregnancy data which were secured included not only an array of objective tests but also personal accounts of feelings and fantasies.

A concise overview of what came out of these inquiries follows.

Menstruation

Two sources of information were available concerning the menstrual behaviour and attitudes of the women who were investigated. One was based on their replies to a number of questions which variously inquired concerning amount of menstrual pain, mood changes associated with menstruation, degree of menstrual irregularity, duration of menstrual flow, and so forth.

A second source was provided by measures taken in several samples of various psychological dimensions during menstruation and also at other times, either before or after menstruation. These measures (for example, Rorschach Ink Blot test, word associations) made it possible to ascertain whether menstruation alters particular aspects of psychological functioning.

It would be well to begin by defining what are the norm or typical menstrual experiences across the samples. The average women in the various samples did not find menstruation to be a very disturbing experience. She reported only mild pain which usually dissipates in about fifteen to sixteen hours; and she indicated experiencing only mild to moderate change in her mood. She also indicated that her onset of menstrual flow is highly regular, typically varying only a few days from the expected date.

The women in one sample were asked to write a personalized account of how they acutually experienced the onset of menstruation. They were instructed:

> Describe briefly what feelings, body sensations, and thoughts you had with the start of your present menstrual period.

They were asked to write their descriptions within a day of the onset of the period. A number of representative excerpts will now be presented in order to illustrate the wide range of reactions and also to point up how relatively well adapted most of the women are to the menstrual events.

Subject 1. I felt quite normal. I knew the day it was expected and it simply came. The only thought I had was that I'm almost out of Tampax and I don't like spending money on something as unexciting as that.

Subject 2. A day or two prior to my period, I begin to wonder 'when' and feel a little insecure because my period will start at any time of day or night without warning and I will just gush forth. This particular period there was relatively no increase in nervous tension. In fact I felt marvellous.

The day prior to the start of my period . . . and the first day of my period there was a great desire for sexual relations on my part – I would say unusual for me, and would attribute this to my general attitude of feeling well, healthy and happy.

Subject 3. Although I usually get some slight advance warning, such as fatigue the day before, this time it came on suddenly (which has also happened before). The first day I was lightly fatigued and had a mild headache part of the day. After the first day I practically never feel anything at all.

Subject 4. No body sensations other than slight cramps. I thought that another month had gone by and I'm not pregnant!

Subject 5. My period started yesterday and I knew it had started because of a feeling of slight pressure. Because I had planned a trip for the time when I normally expect my period, I delayed my period by taking a contraceptive pill for three additional days. I did worry a little about this tactic and wondered if it would have any effect on my period. I didn't expect to delay it till after I returned home. My feelings during my period are the same as any other time. My husband says he cannot tell from my emotional state whether I am menstruating or not.

Subject 6. Except for a few stomach cramps I believe I felt the same. I guess I have a secret desire to be pregnant again. Each month I hope I don't get my period for that reason. It's funny when you think that I take the pills every month faithfully. My period is so slight that it hardly alters my life at all and that is fine with me.

Subject 7. I felt like my body wanted me to calm down. Like all my energies slowed down. I've never had cramps or pain. I become quite emotional and tears flow easily at the slightest wrong or confusion. I compose myself but keep it all inside for a while. I feel a tingling sensation in my thighs in the beginning and become quite bloated and I retain my fluids (like my eyelids, hands). Once in a while in my ankles. I sometimes feel like being completely alone, away from noise, people, phones, and everyone's problems. Once I got one strange sharp pain like a nerve was being pinched through my ovaries. Like a needle pushed through.

Subject 8. I have absolutely no physical feelings with it but I was very glad that it was here because it means I'm not pregnant. I just couldn't handle having a child right now. I guess I feel happier than usual because of this. I'm usually rather depressed but this time it seems as though a great weight has been lifted from my shoulders.

Subject 9. I had gone shopping – when I arrived home I discovered I had begun to menstruate. I was not at all uncomfortable – I had felt extremely tired – that day and the day before. Other than that, I didn't notice any physical change. My moods shift easily at this time – yet I wouldn't say I am depressed. At times I feel edgy!

Subject 10.
1. Once again I was glad that I wasn't pregnant.
2. Wish it would have waited one more day because my husband got back *that* day.
3. More relaxed feeling.
4. First couple of days, I feel the world could fall apart and I wouldn't care.
5. Sometimes I feel my bottom is so heavy that it is going to drop off.
6. Smell sometimes bothers me.
7. Wish I could take a bath morning, noon and evening.
8. Always feel like I am getting cleaned out.

Subject 11. I felt extremely large and heavy. My stomach was very puffy and had a slight amount of stomach cramps and backache. I was relieved when I got my period to know I was safe for one more month, but was also rather disgusted with the whole ordeal. As a matter of fact I dread it. Again I was relieved to have it and start taking pills again.

Subject 12. First reaction that it was exactly on time – as usual – which amazes me how regular the human body can be. It meant relief from the stuffy feeling that I have about two to three days prior to its onset.

Subject 13. The first day brought slight cramps and a wild backache. Aspirin and a night's rest completely eliminated these symptoms. It is usual to feel 'steamy' in the early stage of a period.

This time I felt an extreme fullness as if the flow would be excessive. It is not. The 'fullness' included thighs, as well as abdomen. There was also an excessively warm feeling which usually accompanies the feeling of fullness. This is not synonomous with 'bloat'.

Thoughts were exhilarating, satisfying; much work accomplished – assignments successful.

Subject 14. I had little reaction and a very slight flow. The experience was hardly noticeable except that my breasts were slightly swollen and sore.

Subject 15. My back hurt slightly in the small of it. I get a little happier at the beginning because I suppose it is cleaning me out and I feel this more than some people. Sexually I am more aroused and more easily.

The range of reactions to menstruation is striking. One woman barely notices it. For another it signifies the passage of an additional month in which she did not get pregnant. But for still another it brings disappointment at not having achieved pregnancy. We find too that some are primarily concerned about the inconvenience menstruation introduces by interfering with intercourse. There are others who perceive menstruation largely in terms of it being an unexpected event which can cause embarrassment and arouse disgust. It is further interesting that some are particularly taken with a sense of being cleansed or 'cleaned out' by the menstrual process. In general, the data suggest that the average woman studied reacts to menstruation as a well routinized event which causes some pain and inconvenience, but not a great deal. This is not to deny that there were some extreme cases in which pain and other complaints were quite severe; but even in such instances one is impressed with the acceptance and adaptation which have occurred. The apparent limited impact of menstruation upon the average woman in the samples studied was reaffirmed by the findings which came from comparing scores from many tests obtained during menstruation and at other times (before or after menstruation). They showed that no menstrual versus nonmenstrual differences could be significantly and consistently demonstrated. It was remarkable how similar the menstrual and nonmenstrual scores were.

Let us now address ourselves to the prime question of whether there is a relationship between a woman's sexual response attributes and her *mode* of experiencing menstruation. Without reservation, it can be said that there is little, if any. The measures of menstrual discomfort (for example, pain, mood change) or irregularity were not reliably related to such sexual indices as orgasm consistency or intercourse frequency. They were also not related to how unsatisfied, tired, tense, guilty, embarrassed, strange, or excited a woman feels during and after orgasm. Further, they were not linked to how much a woman prefers clitoral versus vaginal stimulation; the intensity of her orgasms; her degree of satisfaction from masturbation; the degree to which she favours freedom in sexual behaviour; or any of the other sexual indices. It would appear that the manner in which the women respond sexually and feel about sexuality is not predictive of their menstrual discomfort or irregularity. A highly sexually responsive woman seems to have the same probability of finding menstruation painful or irregular as does the woman who is very unresponsive sexually. Interestingly, menstrual discomfort and irregularity were found not to be related to how disturbing a woman recalls her first menstruation to have been to herself or to her parents. They were also unrelated to the way in which she acquired her early knowledge about sex or her recall of how permissive her parents were about sexual matters.

Much information was, of course, available which permitted an evaluation of whether the nature of a woman's menstrual experiences is linked to her personality attributes. However, despite the fact that a formidable battery of personality measures was employed which sampled behaviour at several levels, not a single consistent correlation could be established between menstrual discomfort and personality. Women differing in amount of menstrual discomfort did not differ with respect to such dimensions as degree of femininity, aggressiveness, sociability, passivity, guilt, masochism, and anxiety about sexual themes. It was especially noteworthy that menstrual discomfort was unrelated to measures of anxiety and personal disturbance. The woman who usually operates at a high level of anxiety or tension is not the one likely to feel pain and mood changes during menstruation. There was also no apparent connection between menstrual discomfort and the attributes she ascribed to her parents.

Comment

The results which have been outlined can be succinctly coded into the generalization that the amount of menstrual discomfort and irregularity that a woman experiences bears no relationship to her sexual responsiveness, sexual attitudes, personality traits, or level of anxiety. However, one must immediately introduce the modifying statement that such seems to be true within the limitation of the narrow range of menstrual disturbance found among the samples of married women that were studied. Possibly women who represent more extreme examples of menstrual discomfort or irregularity might be found to be characterized by special sexual or personality attributes. This possibility does not detract from the value of knowing that the variations in menstrual experience which occur within a circumscribed 'normal' range are not linked with sexual or personality or 'mental health' variables. The generally negative findings of the present studies must be given special weight because they are based on rather unique *multiple* samples. Most, if not all, of previous studies in this area have been based on one, or at the most two, samples. The present studies have asked the question of whether there are relationships pertinent to menstrual experiences which will show themselves in repeated trials. A negative reply has presented itself.

Despite the logical appeal of the idea that because menstruation is a function of a woman's reproductive system and sexual behaviour makes use of parts of the sexual anatomy they should be interrelated, the fact remains that such a proposition has been extremely difficult to defend scientifically. Perhaps this is not surprising, if one considers that the present studies have shown that even different aspects of sexual behaviour which might logically have been thought to be linked (for example, orgasm consistency and intercourse frequency) have turned out to be correlated at only a chance level.

Pregnancy

Considerable information was obtained about the relationship of sexual responsiveness to the way in which women experience pregnancy. As mentioned, one sample of women was actually studied both during pregnancy and after delivery of the baby. Many psychological measures were administered at both of these points in time. Analysis of the results indicated few significant psychological changes from the pregnant to nonpregnant states. These findings are congruent with the view which I have expressed in detail in *The Female Orgasm*, that the pregnant woman is not basically in a different psychological state than the nonpregnant woman. This view includes the assertion that the pregnant woman is also not more anxious or psychologically disturbed than the nonpregnant one. This may seem to be a radical assertion, but if one reviews the available scientific literature it seems to be justified.

It was difficult to demonstrate any consistent links between a woman's sexual responsiveness and her mode of response to pregnancy. The highly orgasmic woman did not seem to be less anxious or to have fewer complications during pregnancy than the woman who achieves orgasm only with difficulty. A woman's psychological reaction to being pregnant was similarly not correlated with her actual or preferred intercourse frequencies, her preferences for vaginal as compared to clitoral stimulation, her feelings during and after orgasm, the usual strength of her orgasms, and so forth. It is of further interest that a woman's pattern of adaptation to her pregnancy was not linked with the many different aspects of her personality that were measured. The extremely feminine woman did not adapt better than the less feminine woman. The angry, aggressive woman likewise did not differ from the friendly, sociable one in this respect. The woman with a nurturant, 'giving' orientation could not be differentiated in her pregnancy responses from the egocentric, 'nongiving' woman. Overall, it would be fair to say that there was no consistent evidence that you can tell anything about a woman's sexual behaviour, sexual feelings, or personality traits from the fact that she adapts either well or poorly to the state of being pregnant.

The Delivery Experience

In any analysis of the changes which occur in a woman as she moves from the pregnant to the post-partum state, one must give thought to the effects of the delivery experience itself. How great is the impact upon a woman of what happens to her during the time that her child is being born? One finds that almost nothing is actually known about what happens psychologically in the course of this process. While various observers have described in general terms the nature of the woman's experiences during delivery, little is available in the literature concerning how she actually *feels* and *personally witnesses* it all. Special attention will be devoted to this matter because it is my view that insufficient recognition has been given to the real proportions of the adaptation it requires from the average woman.

It was with the intent of finding out more about the psychological impact of the delivery experience that we asked each of the 49 pregnant women who constituted one sample to write a detailed account of her delivery as soon as possible after the event. The actual instructions to her were as follows:

> As soon as possible after your delivery write several pages in which you describe your experiences. Describe in detail the emotions and body sensations you experienced and also the thoughts and images that passed through your mind.

She was to bring her account of the delivery when she returned to the laboratory for re-valuation one month subsequent to delivery. These accounts proved to be frank and detailed. They provide a rare first-person perspective which really brings home the astonishing vicissitudes of the delivery process. Segments of a representative series will now be presented.

Subject 1. My feelings were immense relief – finally after all these months I was going to have the baby. I prayed that it would be healthy, perfect, and beautiful. I knew the percentage of women having deformed or retarded children wasn't really that large, but nevertheless I was worried that maybe something had gone wrong. Also, since my cramps still weren't very painful, I believe I more than half-convinced myself that I'd be one of the few with a very easy and painless labour and delivery. This being my first baby, I was unprepared for everything . . . The nurses were very nice and helped me to relax. I had thought I'd be terribly embarrassed knowing I would have to be shaved and receive an enema – but realized at the time that this was just a job to the nurses and that there really was no need to be self-conscious . . . The doctor came in and asked me how the pain was. I'll never forget how I felt when the nurse said that my pains hadn't been too bad yet! I thought I was in agony! From about 9.00 p.m. till about 7.30 a.m. that day, I found out that the nurse's remarks were true. I never, never imagined that it would be possible to feel such pain. All I thought about and wanted was the spinal. I could imagine how an addict must feel when he needed a fix. I had been so determined not to yell – but the last three hours – I couldn't care less. I just wanted the shot, wanted someone to help, something that would take the pain away. I remembered the stories of how women said they hated their husbands or hated the baby. I kept thinking that I wouldn't be like that – and even though the pain was unbearable I still was glad about the baby. I really couldn't understand how anyone could blame it on their husbands – after all, I'm sure – even if he'll admit it that he was worried to death. All I wanted was that shot – I kept praying that they'd give it to me. The nurse kept telling me to bear down and not waste the pain – I wondered how many children she had and if she had ever gone through it. Finally my water broke – and they took me into the delivery room.

Subject 2. I was put in a room with two beds separated by a canvas partition. There was a patient in the other bed but she was very quiet. There was also a patient in the labour room across the hall. She was moaning and yelling and I was a little frightened by the sound she made, but more than that I felt disgusted at her behaviour. I told myself that I was not going to behave like that no matter how bad the pains got. During my pregnancy I dreaded the shave prep and enema that I knew I must have in the labour room. However, it was all done so quickly and efficiently that I didn't mind it at all. After a while my pains grew stronger and seemed to be lasting longer. I was given a shot which relaxed me and although each pain seemed unbearable, I knew it would soon go away and I was able to relax and almost sleep in between pains. A doctor came in every once in a while and gave me a rectal examination. This was very painful and I asked him to wait until my contraction passed, but he said he couldn't. When my doctor came in to examine me I felt very relieved to see him. I felt less afraid and was willing to do whatever he said. At this point my doctor and a nurse had me bear down with each contraction. I had to do this about four times and I cried because the pain was so great. They kept making me push and coaxing me and I prayed that it would soon be over. The nurse said she could see my baby and if I would push once more they would take me into the delivery room. The pain seemed constant now, never letting up. I lifted myself onto the operating table and rolled on my side for the anesthesiologist to inject the saddle block into my spine. I waited what seemed a long time but could feel no needle going in me. My doctor told me later the anesthesiologist couldn't get the needle in and that this sometimes happened. I was rolled over and my legs were tied to two bars at the end of the bed. I wanted to push now. The pain made me want to bear down but the nurses told me not to push. I was told to take deep breaths, but this was very difficult; then I was told to pant. I was extremely frightened at this time. A gas mask was put over my nose and mouth and I wanted to pass out. I remember thinking. 'I must be dying. If I am I'll just have to die because I can't stand it any longer.' The gas gave me the effect of being suspended somewhere – not really alive. I could hear deep long moans and I realized they must be coming from me, but I wasn't aware that I was moaning. I had no more pain. I could feel the baby coming out and I felt it stretching me. I had an impulse to close my legs but I couldn't. The next thing I remember is opening my eyes and hearing a baby cry.

Subject 3. I was prepared by my nurse and then my doctor came to examine me. My bag of waters needed to be punctured, so that was my first strange sensation. By that time, lying on my back was very painful, and I found it difficult to concentrate on anything but that each time that it became a necessity. But when my bag of waters was broken my attention was diverted. The puncture itself was somewhat painful, but flow of the warm fluids soothed the pain and felt very good. I am so conditioned to disposing my fluids into the toilet that I felt very strange about lying in a pool of wetness. Later on in the day I had the same feeling when I was unable to control myself and urinated during a contraction. There were so many more important things to think about!

At any rate, the day seemed to be progressing well – I did my breathing exercises and stayed calm during contractions – until the early afternoon. Some time between one and two o'clock the pain started to become unbearable and my cool exterior little by little became undone. Doing the breathing exercises became a chore, and at best I could only do them incorrectly. I wanted very badly to succeed in keeping my head; I didn't want to be a coward. Most of this was because my husband was taking it very hard. I wanted to have him there but not for the purpose of torturing him. Sometime during the afternoon, I am told that I became delirious, failing to recognize people and making little sense when I spoke. I was penetrated twice by hypodermic needles for the pain, had a catheter between my legs, had an intravenous in my hand, was carried off to be X-rayed once, and later in the afternoon had an oxygen mask over my face.

Subject 4. In the wheelchair at the hospital I lost some more water, but not as much as it felt like; I had visions of a water trail behind me and was a little embarrassed about that . . . I changed into the hospital gown, was 'prepped' and then checked rectally – which caused more water to gurgle out. The contractions were still mild . . .

I had taken classes that taught the proper breathing for labour, so I began to breathe with contractions just for practice . . . The doctor tried to check me . . . but my uterus would not cooperate and contract. He wanted to break the water bag more thoroughly, but could not do it without a contraction. He was a jovial doctor, and after holding his finger in my vagina for about five minutes he said his hand was getting tired. He finally gave up, and he told my husband in the waiting room to go home because I was just 'piddling around'.

. . . The contractions began to hurt along the whole lower part of the uterus, as for very strong cramps. I began shallow breathing to relieve the pain. The contractions didn't seem right to me. They hit hard and suddenly, rather than the build-up I had experienced before. Also, I knew them by the lower pain only; my stomach felt flabby and loose to my mind . . . I was too busy 'breathing' to talk to the nurse, but I wasn't good enough at it to look relaxed or comfortable. The pressure rectally and even more so along the front ridge under my stomach became almost unbearable. I felt like crying that I couldn't stand any more and live, but I kept panting and made no noise. (I was also feeling proud that I could at least keep silent.) . . . The doctor arrived in the labour room on time, just barely. I was beginning to lose control of myself. When I was told to sit up for my spinal, I remember whimpering and draping myself like a doll over the nurse.

What heavenly relief with the spinal! The doctor (I think) used a tool to turn the baby before he came out. He had been face up in labour (a more painful position for me). Then out he came, and the doctor got him to cry before plopping him on my stomach. There was a thud of disappointment that it was another boy, and I didn't feel as related to him as I wanted to.

Subject 5. During the night I was examined by doctors several times, until I finally asked them to examine me rectally instead of vaginally, which had become increasingly painful. Labour progressed, but not well enough, so the doctor broke the membranes and some water trickled out. This was not at all painful, and I was continually thankful that he explained everything he was doing and had to do as he went along. This process appeared to stimulate dilation and soon my contractions were every minute or so and exceptionally intense. I have never felt such agonizing pain, and whether it was because I was so tired by this time or because I have a low pain threshold, I began to scream with the severe contractions. I tried to remember how to breathe properly but breathing didn't seem to help. The nurse looked very disapproving and even went next door to explain to the woman labouring there that this was my first baby and I was frightened. I couldn't believe that she was apologizing for me, and I was just steamed and then angry, especially since she didn't try to help me by telling me how to breathe or position myself. The doctor said nothing, just kept his hand on my uterus and encouraged me by his presence. Unfortunately, I was the only one in real labour at this point, and my husband could hear me in the waiting room...

Then suddenly I moved into the second stage of labour and felt an overwhelming desire to push. The sharp searing pains of my earlier contractions gave way to great rolling motions of my uterus which caused me to groan as I exhaled. I remember finding it difficult to catch my breath and being conscious of the tremendous effort I was exerting to push, but being relieved that these contractions *were* endurable. In fact, compared to the end of the first stage of labour, they were actually relaxing. After a great deal of supervised pushing I was transferred to a stretcher and taken to the delivery room and given a saddle block.

Subject 6. Once at the hospital, I was taken directly up to the labour room; my husband accompanied me as far as he could and then waited. I was put into a labour room and given a gown. My pulse, blood pressure, etc., was taken. After this my husband came in to see. As he came in a contraction was just reaching its peak and I could not speak, except in a hoarse whisper. My husband looked absolutely miserable and helpless. I assured him I was all right and he should leave as there wasn't anything he could do. I thought it silly to make him suffer with me, especially when I knew I was capable of taking care of myself. After he left I thought that despite all I had read, no one was really prepared to have a baby.

The nurse came in to shave my pubic hair. She was a jolly, very patient woman. She kept me from constantly thinking about the pain by talking and even joking a bit. Also, she explained the things she did.

Being shaved was very unpleasant; the warm water was nice and the razor didn't pull. It was rather odd to feel the hair be shaved in such an unusual area, but it seemed rather relaxing. When finished the nurse left . . .

The time seemed interminable. Nothing would alleviate the pain and I thought that I hadn't expected or desired this much agony, even though I did want a baby. The nurse then proceeded to give me an enema which was a new, most unpleasant experience. I was prepared for the tube in my rectum, but not for the bloated feeling when the water was forced in. This feeling of fullness increased my pain. I felt absolutely miserable and yet I had to sit on a bedpan to wait on my intestines to empty. Soon the first rush came; it felt like it was just falling out uncontrollably. I found this to be very unpleasant; however, the movements were tolerable, although the pains were not. If anything they seemed worse and were not relievable. I kept my attention focused on the clock as much as possible and when the time was up (the nurse had said it would take about ten minutes) I buzzed for the nurse. Just as she came in I started again which made me feel embarrassed, but she waited calmly until I was through. Then she cleaned me up; I felt sorry for nurses, as I could never stomach having to do such things. Next, she poured some blue, sterile solution over my genital area warning me it would feel cold; however, my body was shocked and jerked a little.

Soon after this my doctor came in. I immediately felt relieved and secure; I knew he would help me. At this time I became only half aware of those around me and more aware of the pain. I found it more difficult to breathe and I wanted to scream. I started moaning loudly and holding my breath and tightening up. My doctor calmed me, telling me to breathe deeply. I did the best I could, for I wanted to make my delivery as easy as possible.

Next I remember seeing the nurse hand my doctor a long piece of metal similar to the dipstick used in a car. With it he broke my water which spurted out forcefully causing everyone to jump back. At this time I noticed the young intern standing at the end of the bed. He was watching me very intently. Our eyes met and we stared at each other for several moments. I felt very strange about him. He appeared to be very curious, yet empathetic and slightly frightened. It is difficult to explain; it seemed he was interested in me, yet aloof.

The pain was now unbearable. I asked my doctor if he could make the pain stop. He said I was going through the worst part, going to the second stage, and that surprisingly things would get better. However, I could not be placated and again asked him to make the pain stop. My doctor now told me to hold my breath and push as hard as I could and that I would be given a shot to ease the pain. I did so, but trying to take a breath seemed to tear me apart. The nurse gave me a shot in the buttocks. I asked how long it would be before the pain would ease and she told me it would take effect in about fifteen minutes, but I would deliver before then. I resigned myself to the fact that the pain would not stop.

Subject 7. The pains started to get very strong. I was in real pain and all of a sudden for the first time I got scared. I knew I was just starting my labour and I couldn't imagine my pains getting any worse. I began to grab on to the sheets as hard as I could, I tried different positions but whatever I did just seemed to make it worse. Finally I pulled myself together after about thirty minutes of twisting and turning. I was once a technician in a programme where I learned the importance of lying as still as possible and trying to relax between and during contractions. So I made up my mind I was going to do it and I was very successful. All I thought about, all I concentrated on was totally relaxing. I wouldn't even allow myself to clench my fist a little. Toward the end of my labour the pain got so bad I felt my entire body was going to explode any second. When I felt a pain starting I would slowly count to myself. I would tell myself by the time I got to ten the pain would be gone. It seemed to help me a little.

At around 6.30 p.m. they told me to start pushing. From then on everything was very easy. Because I relaxed through my labour I had plenty of strength left for pushing. I had the baby's head down in twenty minutes. They brought me into the delivery room where I had a 'natural child birth' (this is what I wanted). From the time they brought me into the delivery room until the time I delivered my baby I felt nothing but complete happiness because I knew the baby was going to be born any minute . . .

Subject 8. I was definitely aware of some kind of inexpressible physical change, but in order to prevent becoming unduly excited and to keep from getting any hopes up for naught, I continued to dismiss the pains as insignificant . . .

By this time I was feeling quite light-headed and very emotional, not really frightened but overawed in anticipation of the monumental event that really did seem on the very brink of occurring now. For a moment I was afraid I would cry, but in the great concentration that was required of me from then on I completely forgot this fear. I was wheeled into a rather stark room, the labour room, containing only a bed and a strange clock which was numbered from one to fifteen and which, I decided, must be for timing contractions. A nurse . . . told me to get undressed and into a gown. My whole being felt numb and unreal except for my abdomen and insides. Nothing of me existed except for the pains. From this point on everything had a dream-like quality. I undressed very awkwardly and gingerly. The nurse listed all of my clothing and possessions on a piece of paper. We discovered that my purse was missing. I couldn't remember whether I'd left it downstairs or in the car. The nurse said they'd call down and have my husband look for it. The missing purse continued to bother me until my husband later told me that he had found it. I was told to lie on the bed where I was shaved . . . Blood pressure was taken frequently from this time until after the birth of the baby. A couple of other nurses were in and out. I was given an enema and sent to the adjoining ladies' room. On top of the labour pains the enema was a very unpleasant experience and I hated every minute of it. I could hear a woman groaning and even screaming somewhere nearby. I was determined not to scream or be cowardly in any way. I walked back to the bed and got onto it. A young, pretty nurse came in. She stayed with me until I went to the delivery room. She timed my pains and talked to me. The pains were very close together now. The nurse explained that soon I would begin to feel like pushing and to tell her when so that she could help me.

Subject 9. The sensations during labour were varied. At times I felt like there was ice on the outsides of my thighs. My body really felt like it was no longer a part of me – I felt somehow disconnected from my body. The 'pains' were feelings of heat or fire in my lower back. I remember consciously counting and breathing deeply during each contraction so as to remain in control of myself. I wanted to remain 'rational'.

I had very few thoughts about the baby itself. I was more concerned that my husband didn't know what was happening.

The most fantastic part of the whole experience was toward the end when the urge to bear down begins. Your body *does* become something apart from you. The urge and the bearing down process is uncontrollable. I distinctly remember thinking during labour that the whole process was ridiculous and I certainly wouldn't be doing it again. It's amazing how this feeling leaves so quickly.

Subject 10. Labour pains were quite severe – I screamed with practically every contraction – I knew screaming wouldn't help the pain any but I still screamed. One nurse scolded me and right then and there I decided I disliked her immensely. I wanted it to be over with. I felt I couldn't take any more. At one time my entire body became numb – my skin prickled – my heart was racing and I felt I was floating in another world. I tried to talk but couldn't. I became frightened. I wanted my husband – I thought I was dying. Apparently I hyperventilated. After what seemed like an eternity I came out of it and I was quite relieved to find out I was still alive. It was the weirdest sensation I have ever felt in my entire twenty-two years.

Subject 11. As the nurse wheeled me down the hall to the labour rooms, all I could think of was that I didn't want to leave my husband. Once in the labour room I started to shake. I was slightly cold but I was really shaking uncontrollably. I admit I was a little nervous but I don't think I was that nervous. Because of this shaking the nurse had a hard time prepping me. All this time I didn't think the labour pains were that hard. After my enema I had to walk to the bathroom; once in there all I could hear was a woman in the next room yelling. This made me very mad because I think all that screaming is unnecessary, plus it seemed to make my pains seem worse. After I got back in bed my labour started to get bad. So I started to kick the guard rails on the bed. Like I said before I don't like screaming so I keep quiet and kick instead. I kicked for quite a while and was just about to ring for the nurse to get me something to help with the pain when she came in; but didn't seem to help . . . When the final stage labour started I was hoping that it wouldn't last too long because I didn't think I could take it without breaking down. Then the nurse came in and checked me, when she said it wouldn't be much longer. I was so relieved that the pain seemed more tolerable. Then all of a sudden I had to bear down and I knew the end was almost near. I knew I wasn't supposed to push so I rang for the nurse. After she checked me she looked at me and said, 'Let's go.' I was so happy and the labour seemed so short . . . It seemed that the nurse was running me down the hall. I could feel the baby coming and all the pain didn't bother me. Next I remember the anesthesiologist coming, he was in a big hurry to get to me. The nurse wanted to check me again but she couldn't because the baby was already there. Then I started asking for my doctor, I was afraid he wasn't at the hospital yet. He was but he was still scrubbing up. I couldn't wait to get the spinal injection because then I knew I could relax and the baby would be born in a few minutes. The spinal took effect fast except for my right leg. It felt like the baby was pressing on a nerve in my leg, the top of my leg seemed cramped, I kept trying to rub it and I wasn't supposed to. So finally the nurse held my hand down. My body felt like it was gently rocking on the table as the doctor pulled out the baby. As I watched the doctor bring out the baby, I asked him what the baby was. He said, 'Here, you can see for yourself.' It was wonderful looking up and seeing your baby that had just been born. I was surprised to find that the baby was a girl . . .

I was anxious to get to recovery so I could see my husband and the baby again. The thing I remember best in recovery was reaching down and feeling my stomach. It was so hollow I couldn't believe it. After visiting with my husband I kept falling asleep. But when I would wake up I kept thinking this must be a dream. It didn't seem possible that it was all over and that I had a beautiful baby girl.

My impressions of all of the delivery reports led me to classify the typical problems faced during delivery, as follows:

1. A major problem is one that is often encountered by any hospital patient. This relates to being placed in a semi-public context where the usual standards of body modesty are abolished and frequent intrusions into one's body are made. The extent to which this occurs with the delivering woman is more extreme than usual because she is repeatedly called upon to expose her genitals, to allow fingers and instruments to be introduced into her vagina and rectum, and finally to be placed in the revealing (and psychologically vulnerable) delivery position (in stirrups) while she is conscious and often in the presence of a variety of others who are largely strangers.

2. Another major problem relates to pain. Not only does the

average woman experience pain greater than that she has ever before encountered, but also it usually persists for an extended period of time. This pain rapidly takes on intolerable intensity and the woman begins to doubt that she can sustain it. She feels that it is 'inhuman' for anyone to be expected to undergo such an experience. She becomes terribly angry about being expected to suffer so unreasonably. She is deeply impressed by the uncontrollable nature of her suffering. She knows there is no way of 'turning off' the birth process once it has started. It should be added that she does know that drugs can relieve her; and is caught in the bind of wanting complete drug-induced relief and yet knowing that sedation will be limited in order to facilitate the birth. Correlated with the experience of being confronted with inevitable pain, one detects a special attitude towards time. Usual standards of time seem to dissolve. There is an overwhelming desire for time to pass instantaneously, but instead it has zero velocity. It becomes a malevolent force.

3. Another problem emphazised by the women in their descriptions is fear of loss of self-control. This fear is initially heightened by the enema usually given after admission to the hospital which produces sensations of being without a functioning anal sphincter. It creates sensations of fluids moving in and out of one's body without any way of regulating them. Other factors which contribute are the breaking of the amniotic sac which results in a gush of leakage; the muscle spasms which surge unpredictably through the body; the persisting unstoppable ('I can't do anything about it') nature of the pain; the occasional loss of bladder control; being surrounded by other women whose cries indicate that they are no longer able to contain their expressions of disturbance; hearing oneself moan and scream despite attempts to inhibit such behaviour; reduced level of consciousness and ego stability resulting from drugs, fatigue, and weakness; and the sensation that body processes are occurring (particularly uterine contractions) which are too powerful to be regulated voluntarily.

4. Finally should be mentioned the build-up of anxiety about possibly sustaining serious injury or death. Few women involved in the painful delivery sequence do not entertain some fantasies that they will be grossly injured ('ripped') or suffer a complication

that will be fatal. Relatedly, it is common to find fantasies that the child to be brought forth will be badly injured or deformed.

There is no question but that a woman is exposed to qualitatively unique and quantitatively intense stresses during the delivery experience. The delivery descriptions which were just presented testify to this convincingly. Is it possible that we have underestimated the seriousness of the damage which may be done to a woman's personality defences and control as the result of the delivery demands? At the very least, they probably leave her unusually vulnerable to other stresses that may be encountered in the first week or two post-delivery.

Besides the descriptions just reviewed, we received from each woman an elaborate series of self-ratings concerning her feelings and attitudes one month following delivery. Also, quite an array of psychological tests were administered to her when she returned to the laboratory after her delivery. Her psychological state in the post-partum phase could therefore be evaluated both in terms of her perception of herself and the scores from the formal tests. It was found that this state was not related in any convincing way to either what was known about her sexual behaviour or her personality. Note particularly that none of the major indices having to do with sexual response, for example, orgasm consistency, feelings during and after orgasm, preference for vaginal versus clitoral stimulation, was correlated with her post-partum psychological condition.

Contraception

Previous Findings

Contraception takes on considerable importance in a woman's life as soon as she begins to have regular sexual intercourse. Improper use of contraception may obviously have serious repercussions for her. There is evidence of considerable irrationality in the way women (and men) choose and utilize contraceptives (Pohlman, 1969). Unsafe contraceptive methods are frequently chosen, or there may be a neglect to employ contraception at all, despite overtly not wanting to become pregnant. Some of this irrationality stems from religious indoctrination (for example, Catholic opposition to formal contraception); some derives from being poorly educated and lacking access to proper information; and some probably represents passive, 'taking-a-chance' behaviour.

Rainwater (1965) has shown too that contraception is least effectively practised in those lower-class families in which the husband and wife have poor communication and are characterized by a 'segregated' relationship in which they 'go their separate ways'. Scattered and inconclusive attempts have been made to relate contraceptive behaviour to other variables like relative dominance of husband and wife (Pohlman, 1969), neuroticism (Lehfeldt and Guze, 1966), degree of personality similarity between husband and wife (Bakker and Dightman, 1964), and personality of the wife (Rodgers and Ziegler, 1968).

It is particularly pertinent to ask whether contraception plays a role in a woman's sexual responsiveness. There are frequent assertions in the literature that fear of pregnancy inhibits women and prevents them from experiencing sexual stimulation positively. Landis, *et al.* (1950) found that women who had one child and who feared becoming pregnant again suffered sexual inhibition as a result of this anxiety. Terman (1938) reported a similar finding, as did Rainwater (1965). Ferber, *et al.* (1966) reported an improvement in sexual responsiveness in a sample in which the fear of pregnancy was banished because the husband had had a vasectomy. These studies seem to be unanimous in their implication that inadequate contraception may arouse anxieties which will interfere with a woman's sexual responsiveness.

However, it must also be reported that an unusually well-designed study of Rodgers and Ziegler (1968), which evaluated changes in sexual behaviour of one sample of couples after the husband had received a vasectomy and in another sample after the wife began using ovulation-suppressing medication for contraceptive purposes, detected no changes in sexual responsiveness as a result of the greater safety from pregnancy which had been thus provided. In both samples interview and questionnaire data were obtained just before the new contraceptive procedures were instituted and follow-up data were then secured for four years. There were no indications that the women in the two samples showed a significant increase in sexual responsiveness or frequency of intercourse as a consequence of their increased immunity from unwanted pregnancy.

One source of irrationality in contraceptive behaviour derives from the fact that some contraceptives require a woman to touch and manipulate her own body and this may arouse anxiety and disturbance. Metzner and Golden (1967) discovered this fact in a study involving one hundred women who were systematically interviewed concerning their contraceptive practices, sexual attitudes, and so forth. The interview also probed specifically concerning the woman's attitude towards the use of intra-uterine devices (IUD). It should be added that a sentence completion test (containing incomplete sentences like, 'Birth control is probably —') was administered to each subject. The analysis of the findings pertaining to which women did and which did not favour the use of IUD's revealed a general difference between them in terms of reluctance to use any contraceptive device requiring vaginal manipulation. To a significant degree, the pro-IUD group exceeded the anti-IUD group in their past use of such vaginal techniques as diaphragm, foam, and suppository. The former group also expressed significantly more positive attitudes than the latter with regard to insertion of other objects (for example, tampons) into the vagina. They were more favourable, too, towards masturbation and sexual intercourse. One may presume, from such findings, that some women either avoid using certain contraceptives or do so in an anxious (inefficient?) manner because they require touching the vaginal area. Apropos of this point, Ellis (1959) describes a patient who owned a diaphragm which she rarely used because it required touching her genitals which were repulsive to her. Relatedly, Rainwater (1960) noted in his interviews with working-class people that they had rather distorted concepts about the consequences of using an intravaginal device like a diaphragm. For example, they feared that it might be 'lost' within the woman's body or that it might produce internal injury.

Rodgers, *et al.* (1965) had fifty married couples rate various contraceptive dimensions (for example, masculine versus feminine, embarrassing versus unembarrassing) and discerned, among other things, that some were perceived as masculine and others as feminine. Thus, the condom is seen as masculine and the dia-

distributed in the diaphragm, foam, intra-uterine device, and condom categories, or some combination of them.

Because rather good information was secured from most of the women that we studied concerning the contraceptives they used, it was possible to probe the issue of whether sexual responsiveness has anything to do with type of contraception used. Does the woman who relies on an oral contraceptive display sexual behaviour different from the woman who does not? Indeed, do women who favour any particular kind of contraception differ in sexual behaviour or attitudes from those favouring any other kind? As defined by the results from the seven samples studied, one can give unequivocal negative answers to all of these questions. The women in the various contraceptive categories were found not to differ from each other in orgasm consistency, actual and preferred intercourse frequencies, clitoral-vaginal preference, feelings during and after orgasm, masturbation frequency or satisfaction, attitudes toward sex freedom, and so forth. Apparently, a woman's sexual response attributes do not result in her selectively choosing one form of contraception over another. It would also seem to be justified to say that continuing use of one form of contraception does not diminish or enhance sexual responsiveness as compared to the continued use of other forms of contraception. These findings might superficially be viewed as not supporting previous studies which reported that fear of pregnancy based on distrust of the form of contraception used inhibited sexual responsiveness. However, one of the questions asked of the women in the various samples was how satisfied they were with their present contraceptive techniques. The great majority indicated it was quite satisfied. The women using oral contraceptives were no more satisfied than those using other forms of contraception. This would imply, then, that the women in the several contraceptive categories did not differ in how 'good' or dependable they regarded their modes of contraception to be. Therefore, they probably did not differ significantly in how anxious they were about the possibility of getting pregnant during intercourse. If so, the present findings that the various contraceptive groups did not differ in sexual behaviour would not bear on previous reports that distrust of a form of contraception can interfere with sexual responsiveness; they would simply indicate that different forms of contraception in which there is equal trust do not affect sexual behaviour differentially.

One other matter that should be mentioned is that there were no consistent relationships between preferred form of contraception and a range of personality and attitudinal measures. In other words, one cannot say that the women who were studied chose one form of contraception versus another because of specific traits, conflicts, or attitudes toward the world. It is likely, instead, that a woman's choice of a contraceptive is strongly influenced by other factors like her husband's preferences, advice given by her gynaecologist, and informal information from friends.

Part II. Conclusions and Interpretations

8. *An Overview of Female Sexuality*

It has become clear that many of our theories and widely accepted ideas about the determinants of female sexual behaviour are probably erroneous and need revision. Hopefully, the revision can be accomplished by scientific observation and reason. The pressure for such revision comes not only from scientific tradition but also from the practical importance of making available accurate information about sexuality. A tremendous volume of pseudo-fact is being transmitted to people of all age levels about the nature of sexual response; and one would guess that this encourages irrational behaviour in the sexual domain. This point applies doubly to the behaviour of many professionals (psychoanalysts, counsellors) who have subjected patients and others seeking help to unreasonable expectations about how they should behave sexually. The need for making available accurate information about sexuality is dramatized when one finds, upon scanning the existing literature, that no scientific reports are to be found about exactly how the majority of persons go about having sexual intercourse. Actually we still know little about the specific kinds and amounts of foreplay employed; their sequence; the emphasis placed on direct clitoral versus vaginal stimulation; and the relative timing of each partner's orgasm. In other words, what occurs during intercourse in the average instance has remained somewhat obscure. This is particularly true if one asks questions about the typical feelings and fantasies that are aroused during intercourse. Intercourse as a psychological phenomenon has not been studied scientifically.

This chapter will be devoted to pulling together the conglomeration of information about sexual responsiveness in women which has accumulated. Earnest efforts will be made to bridge between the work of previous investigators and the findings of the present studies. Broad generalizations about the nature of female sexuality will be offered. Also, answers will be formulated to a variety of questions concerning factors which play a role in a woman's sexual behaviour and attitudes.

The Female Sexual Potential

It would be well at this point to discredit long extant beliefs concerning woman's inferiority in experiencing sexual stimulation and also to challenge the supposition that she has an inferior concept of her own sexual attributes. Masters and Johnson (1966) have already presented evidence that a woman's orgasm is physiologically analogous in many ways to that of the man. They have also found that women are potentially capable of having a greater number of orgasms per unit time than men can. However, despite this fact there are two ideas which persist which portray women as sexually inferior in a psychological sense. One of these ideas, which was partially energized by Kinsey, *et al.* (1953) is that women are less sexually aroused than men by psychosexual stimuli; particularly if they are visual in nature. It is asserted, for example, that pictures depicting nudity or sexual themes evoke relatively little sexual response from women; and the implication has been therefore drawn that women are less sexually arousable (less sensitive to sexually stimulating things) than men. The second of these ideas, which was given a pseudo-scientific rationale by Freud, is that a woman typically has a negative attitude toward her own body because she sees it as inferior to the phallic body of the man. Presumably, she feels deprived or 'castrated' because she lacks that superior organ, the penis. The underlying assumption has been that having a vagina rather than a penis is a badge of inferiority and a cause for disturbance. It is not an exaggeration to say that Freud pictured the young female child as merely a castrated version of the male child. The view has been widely propagated that a woman experiences her body in a more disturbed and unsatisfied fashion than a man does. These two ideas just presented reverberate in many other notions about the psychological sexual inferiority of the woman. For example, one can find assertions that sexual arousal is less important to women than to men; or that the orgasm experience is a more 'natural' thing for men than for women; or that women fre-

phragm as feminine. One of the chief determinants of whether a device is classified as masculine or feminine is whether the man or woman has control of, and responsibility for, it. Both Rainwater (1965) and Pohlman (1969) point out the irrationality in contraceptive behaviour that may arise as the result of the obligations and demands made upon either a wife or husband as a function of the 'masculine' or 'feminine' quality of the contraceptive they employ. A wife who uses the diaphragm may resent the burden of deciding whether to insert the diaphragm each night because it implies a decision as to whether intercourse will take place. If she delays inserting the diaphragm until its need is apparent, her husband may become angry at the delay and inconvenience occasioned by the interruption. Clearly, there is the potential for considerable misunderstanding and role conflict. If a 'masculine' form of contraception is used (condom), a woman may feel particularly insecure (and therefore unresponsive) because she has no direct control over what is done and has to trust that her partner is adequately protecting her. Her partner may sense her distrust and this may in turn influence the efficiency with which he applies the contraceptive device.

Some of the factors which might possibly determine whether a contraceptive will be acceptable to a particular husband-wife pair is illustrated by the observations of Rodgers and Ziegler (1968). They studied thirty-nine couples (by means of interview and psychological tests) prior to their use of an oral contraceptive; and subsequently followed up their behaviour for four years after use had begun. Fifteen of the couples continued to use the oral contraceptive during the four-year period; but nine discontinued without any obvious logical rationale for doing so. Rodgers and Ziegler were interested in possible differences between such 'continuous' and 'discontinuous' couples. They found, particularly on the basis of psychological tests, that the 'continuous women are generally more socially competent, self-satisfied, and independent than are the discontinuous women' (p. 588); and they obtained lower femininity scores than the discontinuous. Further, the same tests indicated that the husbands of the continuous women were less 'concerned about avoiding criticism than are their discontinuous counterparts'; and also less 'conscientious about fulfilling their own social role obligations' (p. 589). When the attributes of husband and wife were compared, it was found that the use of the oral contraceptive was most likely to be continued in a marriage in which the wife had relatively more ascendant traits. One could interpret such a finding in the context of the fact that the oral contraceptive requires the woman to take prime responsibility. She must monitor herself and make sure that she takes the pill at specific points in time. Perhaps a woman who is low in ascendancy and who avoids assuming obligations becomes uncomfortable with the burdens placed upon her by the responsible role linked with the use of an oral contraceptive.

During their study, Rodgers and Ziegler became impressed with the complex interplay of motives between a husband and wife as they seek out a form of contraception which will be acceptable to both. While they remarked that it is usually the one who is most 'conscientious' and who tends to assume 'ambiguous role responsibilities' who is also most likely to take the responsibility for contraception, they pointed out other potential complications that may develop. For example, a wife may reject the use of the oral contraceptive not because she is a person who usually tries to evade responsibility but rather because it results in sexual relations more frequently than she prefers. She may want a form of contraception which will make her less continuously sexually available or which will make it possible for her to use the excuse of fear of pregnancy as a reason for limiting intercourse frequency. This motive may cause her to exaggerate the side effects of an oral contraceptive and to declare them intolerable. It should be added, by way of a note of caution, that although there were individual cases in which degree of interest in sexuality seemed to play such a part in contraceptive behaviour, it was *not* possible to demonstrate in the sample studied an overall significant relationship between continuing the use of the pill and intensity of sexual interest.

Present Findings

About 50–60 per cent of the women whom we studied were relying on an oral contraceptive. The remainder were about equally

quently cannot enjoy sex (and being a woman) because of 'penis envy'.

The actual facts do not support notions about women's sexual deficiencies. Consider for a moment the idea that women are less aroused than men by psychosexual stimuli. With an increasing influx of relevant information (for example, Sigusch, *et al.*, 1970), it is becoming obvious that women do respond with excitement to all kinds of psychosexual stimuli, including visual ones. While there are *overall* average trends for men to report slightly more sexual excitement than women to pictures depicting nudity, it is also true that there are many individual women who report more excitement than do many men. Actually, some women have reported a level of excitement which is attained by few men. One must keep in mind, too, that it is deceptive to compare the averaged reports of men and women concerning the excitement evoked in them, because cultural standards disapprove of women talking as openly as men about experiencing sexual excitement. Probably, as it becomes more respectable for a woman to say that even nontraditionally romantic sexual material excites her, the small average differences between the reports of women and men with respect to amount of sexual arousal evoked by visual stimuli will disappear from research studies.

Let us appraise, too, the widely accepted stereotype that the average woman perceives her body as sexually inferior to that of the man; and consequently finds it a source of discomfort and anxiety. The scientific findings overwhelmingly contradict this concept of female inferiority. One can, on the contrary, make out a good case for the assertion that men are more insecure and anxious about their bodies than women are. There are several lines of evidence which point in this direction. Scientific findings indicate (Fisher, 1970) that men have more anxiety than women about possibly sustaining body damage: they have more fantasies about body injury and seem to be more threatened by situations (for example, hospitalization) with special body implications. They even dream more about body injury than do women. There is also evidence they have less clearly defined body boundaries than women; and this suggests that they feel relatively more concerned about outside forces possibly intruding upon their bodies. Further, one should mention that men seem less comfortable than women about focusing attention upon their own bodies. It is acceptable that a woman should lavish interest on her body and experiment with its adornment; but a man who behaves equivalently is viewed with suspicion. Such differences in body attitudes between women and men have been described by a number of researchers. Interestingly, they have been detected even in early childhood. One is reminded that some observers (Katcher and Levin, 1955; Katcher, 1955) report that girls arrive at a realistic notion of the difference between masculinity and femininity and also between female and male genitals earlier than boys.

It was my conclusion, after reviewing all available studies, that the average woman is more 'at ease' with her own body than is the average man. She not only feels less body threat but can more clearly see a relationship between her body and her primary life roles. As Douvan and Adelson (1966) and others have shown, most young women still *primarily* have the goal of marrying and becoming a mother. A woman can easily discern a link between the sexual and reproductive aspects of this role and the related aspects of her own body. Her body 'makes sense' to her as one of the prime means to become what she wants to become. This is probably much less true for the man. Many of his most important life goals revolve about attaining vocational success and often these goals call for activities which require little body strength or prowess. The businessman or the lawyer or the clerk cannot conjure up much of a logical connection between his body attributes and his vocational identity, which for most men is basic to self-definition. The woman can more easily integrate her body meaningfully into the pattern of her life than the man can. It is the man, rather than the woman, who is more likely to feel insecure about his body and alienated from it.

There is no factual basis for regarding women as psychologically less sexually secure or able than men. To continue to promulgate ideas about such alleged inferiority would seem to be an expression of anti-female prejudice.

What Determines How Sexually Responsive a Woman will Be?

There is no question that the women we studied were 'sexually responsive'. While a sizeable percentage did not attain orgasm *consistently* during intercourse, it was also true that, on the average, they experienced their sexual encounters positively. The average woman enjoyed intercourse and considered the sexual dimension of her life to be a major source of gratification. She did not find intercourse painful; and was not particularly concerned about getting hurt or becoming unexpectedly pregnant when she was vaginally penetrated. She spent quite a bit of time thinking about sex and preferred to have intercourse with considerable frequency. She did not feel that her husband was making inordinate sexual demands upon her. After orgasm she described herself as feeling satisfied, happy, and relaxed. A picture emerges in which sexual stimulation and all that is associated with it have a clear positive valence in the lives of the married women who were studied. Sex was largely perceived by them as a source of fun and enjoyment. This positive picture contrasts with the rather grim and negative portrayals found in many clinically oriented sources. Some writers have depicted the sexual life of the average woman as a maze of difficulties, conflicts, and threatening consequences. Of course, one could object that the samples we studied are hardly representative of women in general; and it could be argued that studies of women from lower socio-economic groups would uncover more negative attitudes. This cannot be denied and one will have to suspend judgement until data equivalent to ours are obtained from other strata of the culture. But it should be added that other studies of middle-class women (for example, Ard, 1962; Terman, 1938) have also found that, on the average, such women regard sexual transactions as enjoyable. Schaefer (1964) reported that even in a sample of troubled women who had sought psychotherapeutic treatment sexual gratification was a significant component of life. While the marital sexual relationship is a complicated one and often calls for new adaptations, it apparently is very rewarding to many.

Obviously, one cannot really treat sexual responsiveness as a unitary entity. There are many ways of defining what happens during a sexual interaction. Sexual stimulation has complex effects and each individual may selectively focus on one effect as compared to another. Sexual arousal can stir up a variety of fantasies; it may or may not eventuate in orgasm; the orgasm itself may be strong or weak; the orgasm may be enjoyable or even unenjoyable; the orgasm may be followed by relaxation or even by increased tension; there may be no orgasm but the unresolved build-up of sexual excitement may somehow be an intriguing experience; the closeness of one's body to the sexual partner may be more prominent in awareness than the orgasm attained; and so forth. Not only do different women have different ways of enjoying (and not enjoying) sexual stimulation, but also it is probable that they individually fluctuate to some extent in their own pattern of enjoyment over a series of sexual contacts. The psychological complexity of sexual arousal in a woman cannot be overemphasized. It is too easy to slip into simplistic notions that women are neatly ordered into 'sexy' and 'non-sexy' categories. The real complexity of the matter can perhaps best be conveyed by stating that one can easily accept the possibility that there are instances in which the extremely 'sexy' woman who always achieves intense orgasms may not get as much satisfaction out of intercourse as the apparently less 'sexy' woman whose orgasms are inconsistent and of lesser strength. Measures of different aspects of the response to sexual stimulation either do not correlate with each other, or, if they do, the correlations are of low magnitude. A woman may be high in terms of one index of responsiveness and low in terms of another. She may obtain much satisfaction from orgasm but *prefer* to engage in intercourse infrequently. She may rarely attain orgasm and still *actually* have a high intercourse rate. Whether she attains orgasm may be unrelated to most of the qualitative sensations that she has during orgasm (for example, feeling tense or depersonalized).

When referring to a woman's sexual responsiveness, care needs to be taken to specify a particular aspect or dimension. One can refer to her orgasm consistency or her intercourse frequency or her likelihood of feeling 'ecstatic' during orgasm or the frequency of intercourse she prefers or the number of different intercourse positions she uses, but one would rarely be able to make the statement that she is *generally* high or low with respect to most of these dimensions. While a conclusion of this sort may appear to be unreasonable when applied to sexual behaviour, it would not seem so if applied to another kind of appetite, such as eating. The average person's 'responsiveness' to food could probably not be adequately described by terms like 'high' or 'low'. One may like food a great deal and yet eat only small quantities; or one may intensely enjoy a narrow spectrum of foods and dislike most others; or one may relish eating but begin to feel discomfort from it when the digestive processes get under way; or one may get more satisfaction from the social context of eating than from the food itself; and so forth. This general perspective does not mean that certain aspects of sexual responsiveness cannot be viewed as being relatively more important than others. There is probably little question that the average woman places high value during intercourse on becoming highly excited, attaining orgasm, and finally arriving at a feeling of satisfaction. She probably also attaches a fair amount of importance to the frequency with which she engages in intercourse. Certain aspects of sexual arousal may, on the contrary, be ascribed low importance. In all likelihood, the average woman engaging in regular intercourse does not attend to whether her orgasm is of extremely high as compared to moderate intensity; is not terribly concerned about the matter of multiple orgasms; and does not have a large investment in using many as compared to few intercourse positions.

Attainment of orgasm is one of the prime ways of defining sexual responsiveness. This is true despite the often discussed fact that there are other important feelings and sensations linked with intercourse which, in individual cases, may be even more important than the orgasm itself. In general, orgasm is a major criterion of sexual responsiveness, whether one evaluates it from the private perspective of the individual's own feelings or that based on more public norms and expectations. Because it is assigned so much importance, as compared to other kinds of feelings and sensations, there has been surprise, amounting almost to consternation, at the repeated research findings that about 30 per cent of all married women either do not ever attain orgasm or do so only occasionally. These findings have been interpreted by some to mean that a large segment of women in our culture do not get very aroused by, or really enjoy sexual stimulation. Observations from our studies would argue that this is an overstatement. The women in the various samples did generally value sexual stimulation and did assign considerable importance to it in their lives, despite their not infrequent difficulties in achieving orgasm. But there still remains the puzzling question as to why so many women lack the ability to mass their excitement to the orgasm threshold. One of the most popular explanations is that many women are brought up puritanically and have so much anxiety and inhibition about sexual matters that they respond negatively when exposed to sexual stimulation. A second places the burden of failure upon the male partner who is portrayed as inadequate in his sexual approach: he is said to be too aggressive and shocking in his sexual behaviour; or not willing to deliver sexual stimulation for a sufficiently sustained period; or not bestowing it in the correct proportions to certain anatomical areas as compared to others (for example, clitoral versus vaginal).

The explanation based on puritanical upbringing is difficult to sustain in the face of several contradictory facts. First of all, no one has been able to detect a convincing link between orgasm consistency and religiosity, except perhaps in a few extreme instances. Terman (1938, 1951) could find no significant correlations between orgasm indices and measures of religiosity (such as church attendance, religious affiliation); and this was essentially true also in the Kinsey, *et al.* (1953) study (except for a small extremely devout Catholic sample). It will be recalled too that we failed to find a significant correlation, across numerous samples, between orgasm consistency and indices of religiosity. The 'puritanical' hypothesis is further contradicted by our findings that a woman's recall of how permissive or repressive her parents had been about sex does not correlate with orgasm consistency. It is additionally pertinent that several studies (including ours) have shown that the extent to which a woman recalls her parents as having personally participated in giving her sexual information is quite unrelated to her sexual responsiveness. The 'puritanical' hypothesis would, on the contrary, lead one to expect that since parents who refrain from giving information about sex probably are inhibited about sexuality, their children would have difficulties in sexual interactions.

Other measures of sexual enjoyment (for example, satisfaction after orgasm, self-rated sexual responsiveness) have also turned out to be unrelated to recall of how one's parents behaved with respect to sexual matters. A woman's ability to be sexually responsive is apparently not linked with the adequacy of the sex information provided by her parents; how openly they talked to her about sexual matters; their attitudes about nudity and the display of one's body; their degree of open display of affection toward each other; their reaction to the onset of her menstruation; and so forth. In other words, there is no empirical support for the idea that the parents' *formal* or *explicit* behaviour with regard to sexual matters has a profound effect upon their daughter's psychological sexual development. The parent who is open about sexual matters and who provides explicit sexual information is no more likely to produce a daughter without sexual-response difficulties than the parent who is reserved in communications about sex. Such observations raise questions about the emphasis which some have placed upon the importance of the parent providing formal instruction about sexual matters to their children. Formal information about sex may facilitate certain aspects of adaptation to sex role, but on the basis of the presently available findings one would have to be sceptical that such information will make a fundamental difference in a woman's ability to enjoy sexual stimulation.

The notion that a woman's orgasm difficulties reflect her husband's poor love-making techniques also does not stand up well against the available research evidence. The extensive studies by Terman (1938, 1951) in which wives and their husbands were evaluated in detail turned up few, if any, consistent correlations between diverse husband attributes (including sexual behaviour) and wife's orgasmic ability. It is also true that Kinsey, *et al.* (1953) and others have generally been unable to show that a woman's orgasm consistency is related to several different aspects of the husband's sexual behaviour (for example, how long he persists in applying sexual stimulation to his wife). In our studies there were no consistent correlations between variables which certainly reflect the husband's sexual behaviour (number of intercourse positions, amount of foreplay, duration of sexual stimulation) and the wife's orgasm consistency. However, such findings are not meant to imply that a husband's particular pattern of sexual behaviour does not importantly affect the content and 'feel' of his wife's sexual experiences, but only that it does not play a decisive role in whether she will reach orgasm. The probable picture which emerges is that, beyond the point of delivering a certain necessary minimum of stimulation, the husband's *sexual* behaviour is of secondary importance as to whether his wife will build up to orgasmic excitement. At a later point, the potential role of the husband's personality in this orgasmic process will be further considered. Of course, there can be no certainty on this matter until other studies are done in which more detailed information is obtained about male sexual behaviour and its effect on female orgasm.

Let us review the factors which have been shown to be correlated with a woman's orgasm consistency. The results of our studies will first be considered. One of the primary findings was that the greater a woman's feeling that love objects are not dependable (that they are easily lost or will disappear) the less likely she is to attain orgasm. Women with orgasm difficulties were found to produce an elevated number of ink-blot and story themes referring to death and separation. Also, there was actual evidence that such women are likely to have suffered the literal loss (through death) or functional loss (due to long periods of absence from home) of father during childhood. These and related findings were explained in terms of a model which focuses upon the blurring of consciousness and the diminished 'hold' upon what is 'out there' by a woman as her sexual excitement mounts to the point of orgasm. It was theorized that the woman who feels that objects are undependable and who fears their loss finds the blurring of her relationships with objects which is produced by sexual excitement so threatening that she has to 'turn it off'. Presumably, she is made so uncomfortable by the loss implications of her excitement that the process of building up to orgasm is inhibited or blocked.

It is essential to add that the concern about loss of objects is not a sign of personality disturbance. That is, there was no indication that women who do not attain orgasm consistently are *generally* more anxious or in poorer 'mental health' than women who do reach orgasm consistently. Concern about loss of objects may be viewed as one problem among many other kinds of psychological difficulties that afflict humans; and need be neither more nor less burdensome than other varieties of problems. Further, one may suggest that although a woman is especially concerned about object loss she can still learn to cope with it via compensatory defences, which would make it possible for her to function just as well as persons without such concern in most contexts (with the exception of situations involving build-up of sexual excitement). The fact that we did not find greater *general* psychological disturbance in low- as compared to high-orgasmic women certainly fits with the majority of previous studies in which there has been failure to demonstrate that a woman's sexual responsiveness has anything to do with how psychologically disturbed she is. There is, for example, no consistent evidence in the literature that schizophrenic women are less sexually responsive than those who are nonschizophrenic. It is doubtful that the myth that orgasm consistency reflects mental health will die easily. The psychiatric literature is saturated with belief in this concept, it has been perpetuated by endless anecdotes and case studies, and has become an article of faith. One would guess that if observers had been as alert to detect exceptions to the equation between orgasm ability and psychological disturbance as they were to amass support for it, the clinical literature would now contain as many negative as positive reports. There is really no persuasive reason for viewing low-orgasm consistency in a woman as just another example of her general inability to cope adequately with the world. Such a view only perpetuates the stereotype that a woman's orgasm capacity is an index of her general superiority-inferiority as a functioning person. If analogous reasoning were applied to a woman's enjoyment of eating or sleeping or physical exercise, it would evoke only amusement.

It is even possible to propose speculatively that certain kinds of disturbance in psychological functioning might facilitate orgasm. If it is assumed that the increasing excitement which leads to orgasm becomes ultimately inhibiting to many women because it causes a threatening blurring of their perceptual 'hold' on objects, the question arises whether those who have had previous 'practice' with such blurring experiences might be less threatened by them. One way in which 'practice' of this kind might have been obtained would be via previous psychopathological experiences. A woman who has had, over the years, to cope with the impact of intense anxiety or with psychotic-like distortions of the world might gradually adapt to the experience of having a tenuous 'hold' on objects. The blurring of perception produced by sexual excitement would, then, be a familiar phenomenon to her; and so there might be a lower probability that it would have an acute disturbing or inhibiting effect. Such a formulation could possibly help to explain puzzling reports in the clinical literature about certain schizophrenic women who appear to be unusually orgasmic. Perhaps some schizophrenic women are able to derive from this history of fluid and fluctuating reality contact the 'skill' to immerse themselves in, and let themselves be carried away by, other varieties of experiences which blur contact with objects. They would therefore not be particularly alarmed by alterations in perception which are caused by intense sexual arousal. Of course, this immediately raises the question as to whether women who have had histories of epileptic seizures or who have intensively cultivated the use of consciousness-altering drugs experience the perceptual blurring of sexual excitement as an old, familiar phenomenon. If so, how does it affect their orgasm potential? In effect, what I propose is that while confidence in the stability of love objects may be the principal facilitator of orgasm, there may be a paradoxical opposing familiarity with the instability of consciousness which can also facilitate orgasm. While it may turn out that only a relatively small percentage of women become highly orgasmic via the instability route, it is a matter of considerable theoretical importance which should be studied.

Another point that needs underscoring is that orgasm consistency was found *not* to be related to a host of variables which have often been cited in the literature as contributing to 'frigidity'. For example, orgasm consistency turned out not to be related to degree of femininity (as conventionally defined), attitudes towards mother, aggressiveness, passivity, guilt, religiosity, recalled attitudes of parents towards sex, impulsivity, narcissism, and so forth. One cannot glibly speak of orgasm as more likely to occur in women with certain personality traits as compared to others. The likelihood of orgasm is no greater in the forceful than the passive, in the feminine than the not-so-feminine, in the sociable than the shy, in the extroverted than the reflective, in the self-centred than the altruistic, in the conservative than the liberal, and in the calm than the anxious. What has emerged from my findings is that orgasm consistency tends to be diminished in women with a particular kind of uncertainty about people (that people cannot be depended upon to remain available for relationships). However, this type of uncertainty can apparently exist in women of diverse personalities. One would presume that there are potentially an infinite number of ways in which it can be dealt with, contained, and expressed.

If it has not already become obvious, it should be pointed out that the concept of fear of loss of love object bears a remarkable resemblance to the concept of fear of loss of love or separation from love object which has been found to be a type of anxiety particularly characteristic of women. While concern about body damage has been found to typify men, women have been observed in several studies (for example, Bradford, 1968) to be especially sensitive to potential separation from those with whom they have close relationships. This sensitivity has been detected in their responses to questionnaires about the kinds of things they fear. It has also evidenced itself in the themes of stories they create and in brief samples of their stream-of-thought. Bradford (1968) stated (p. 88):

> It might be argued that from infancy on, females are encouraged to be people and home oriented; that parents tend to use withdrawal of love rather than physical punishment in disciplining girls and thus their extreme sensitivity to this threat ...

One cannot help being impressed with the fact that a species of anxiety which has been identified in the literature as typifying women should turn out to be a significant element in interfering with their attainment of orgasm. If Bradford is correct in his statement that threatened withdrawal of love is one of the common ways of disciplining girls, it would follow that an 'anti-orgasm' vector is built right into the current modal style of rearing girls.

Perhaps this accounts for the high frequency with which orgasm difficulties are encountered in women. It is a paradox that the very socialization experiences which give rise to certain aspects of what we call a female orientation may simultaneously be generating an incapacity to cope with the conditions associated with orgasmic levels of excitement. If there are any cultures in the world in which the socialization of the girl does not involve focusing her anxieties upon potential separation from love objects, they would provide a unique opportunity to evaluate the role of fear of loss of love objects upon orgasm consistency. Obviously, one would expect orgasm consistency rates to be unusually high in such cultures. I would urge that cross-cultural studies pertinent to this matter be given high priority.

Relevant to this same issue, I think that even *within* our culture it might be possible on the basis of an analysis of child-rearing practices to demonstrate changes over the last several generations in the degree to which girls are instilled with anxiety about separation from love objects. If so, one would conjecture that it would be found that there has been a gradual decline in the practice; and so there should be a perceptible parallel increase in orgasmic consistency. One is reminded, in this respect, that Kinsey, *et al.* (1953) reported that orgasm consistency rates for married women were higher in those born after 1900 than before that date, and in fact show a trend to increase in succeeding generations after 1900.

If concern about loss of love objects does, actually, contribute to a woman's orgasmic difficulties, does this not raise the possibility that the behaviour of her sex partner, who is, after all, one of the most important in the class of current 'love objects', may also be significantly involved? This question is asked in the face of the fact that previous intensive studies (for example, Terman, 1938, 1951) have not been able to demonstrate that a wife's orgasmic capacity is correlated in any noteworthy way with the attributes of her husband. These studies have examined not only reports of the sex behaviour of the husband but also measures of his personality, social status, and so forth. Even so, one must question whether they concerned themselves sufficiently with patterns of husband behaviour which might particularly affect a woman's feelings about loss of sex object. For example, since men probably also vary in their anxiety about potential loss of love objects, is it possible that a husband with high concern of this kind might reinforce an analogous concern in his wife – and in so doing decrease her orgasm consistency? But if his anxiety about object loss were unusually low he might also communicate this feeling to his wife and in the process give her reassurance which would counter her own uncertainties about loss. Perhaps a husband can intensify or decrease his wife's concern about object loss in terms of how much his work keeps him away from home or how often he communicates in an empathic fashion with her or the degree to which he expresses anger by sulking and going off by himself rather than openly ventilating it. Such behaviour patterns and others of a related order are difficult to measure and one can definitely say that they have not been adequately evaluated in previous studies of how husband's attitudes and wife's orgasm consistency are correlated. It would seem to be sensible at this point to suspend judgement about the husband's potential impact, via his general conduct and emotional stance, upon certain of his wife's emotional attitudes which probably influence her orgasmic potential. Apropos of this matter, one is reminded that Masters and Johnson (1970) state that successful treatment of a woman with orgasmic problems requires that she be seen conjointly with her husband (as a 'unit'). They see the husband as playing a significant part in helping his wife to overcome orgasm inhibitions. It should be cautioned that this view is based on clinical observation and still awaits empirical support.

An earlier described review of the literature indicated that, with increasing education or increasing social class, women show greater orgasm consistency. Kinsey, *et al.* (1953) have detected such positive correlations between orgasm consistency and both social class and education. These correlations may indirectly support my formulation that concern about object loss interferes with orgasm. One can reason that, the more limited a woman's education or the lower her social class the more likely she is to have come from an economically deprived background in which uncertainty about loss would be magnified. This uncertainty might stem from the greater probability of occurrence of such events as sudden loss of family income, desertion by father, and serious illness among family members. The lower socio-economic family context is one in which there is less assurance that one's parents will be able to provide necessary resources and that they will remain consistently available for relationships. Chronic exposure during childhood to unpredictability might instill the sort of concern about loss of objects which has been found to be correlated with low-orgasm consistency.

It must be reiterated that not a particle of data has been uncovered which would indicate that the likelihood of being orgasmic is a function of rate of physiological maturation or gross physical attributes. Orgasm consistency is, for example, not correlated with age of menarche and age of development of axillary or pubic hair. It is also not related to indices of body size (for example, height, weight, breast size); and menstrual characteristics (namely, irregularity, duration of flow). Those researchers who have evaluated the evidence with respect to the influence of hormonal factors on the sexual responsiveness of women have not been able to discern convincing relationships. Generally, it can, with justification, be said that no convincing relationships have as yet been established between orgasm consistency in women and specific physiological or constitutional factors. This does not, of course, rule out the possibility that there really are such factors or that genetic influences may be of some importance. However, the burden of proof rests upon those who would appeal to them as explanatory concepts.

A key question that arises in discussing a woman's orgasm consistency concerns how early in her development it is determined. Do her childhood relationships with her parents already define whether she will be 'high' or 'low'? Are the early years of her heterosexual liaisons of crucial importance? Is the whole process actually unpredictable because single dramatic or traumatic events (such as first intercourse experience) have large impact? If childhood relationships are important, to what degree can their influence be altered by adult love relationships and adult sexual experiences? These are the questions that one would like to be able to answer. They cannot all be fully and adequately dealt with on the basis of our current knowledge, but there is a fair amount of information which permits partial replies. First of all, it seems fair to say that there are research findings which indicate that early interactions with parents do play a role in a woman's later ability to be orgasmic. These findings specifically involve relationships with father. Our studies indicated a trend for a woman's orgasm consistency to be positively correlated with her recall of how demanding and definite (as contrasted to casual and permissive) her father's expectations of her had been. If one accepts the fact that her perception of her father's behaviour towards her mirrors, to some extent, how he treated her as she was growing up, one would have to conclude that already during childhood she was having social experiences which would influence her later orgasmic potential. If one had to speculate what she was learning from these interactions with her father, it would be that he was sufficiently seriously interested in her as a person to expend a good deal of energy in guiding and helping her to structure her life. If he was obviously seriously interested in guiding her, she could, even if she resented his authoritarianism and his intrusiveness, feel that he was *dependably* invested in her. Incidentally, the fact that a woman's perception of equivalent qualities in her mother was found not to be correlated with her orgasm consistency suggests that it is particularly the father's dependability which is important in shaping her orgasm potential. The most obvious way to explain this differential would be to point to the fact that her orgasm potential does, after all, express itself in her interactions with a male sex partner; and so it would be logical that her feelings about the dependability of the prime male figure in her early life should be the specific ones to carry over to her later sexual relationship with men. In any case, all that we can say is that to some significant but unknown degree the nature of a woman's transactions with her father as she is growing up will probably affect her orgasm capacity. Because of the imperfect techniques available for measuring the variables involved, one cannot begin to define realistically how influential these early transactions are. They could be enormously important and even *the prime determinant* of orgasmic potential. This remains to be seen.

Indeed, one is tempted to ascribe great importance to this kind of early socialization influence because there have been so few, if any, other influences which have shown even a hint of a link to orgasm consistency. In earlier chapters it was noted that there is little evidence that the average woman's orgasm potential is shaped by one or a few special traumatic sexual episodes. For example, unmarried women who find it necessary to obtain an an abortion, which would certainly be a severe traumatic event, do not later, in their first year of married intercourse, show lowered orgasm consistency. Women who report childhood episodes in which they were raped or forcefully seduced are not less orgasmic than women who indicate they did not suffer in this fashion.

I could find no consistent correlations in our data between orgasm consistency and how a woman experienced such major sex development landmarks as first menstruation, first serious date, and first intercourse. Those who recalled their first intercourse as extremely unpleasant were no less orgasmic than those who remembered it as very pleasant. The temptation to minimize the influence of actual sexual learning experiences, as such, upon orgasm capacity is encouraged by the findings, across several studies, that a girl's dating history gives no hint as to her orgasm consistency. How early a girl begins to date or the average frequency with which she dates at different phases of her adolescence and early womanhood or the seriousness of her dating (as defined by 'getting engaged') do not foretell her orgasm behaviour. This was apparent in Terman's (1938, 1951) data and also those of the writer and others. Whatever a girl learns about heterosexual behaviour and about relating to a male intimately from her dating experiences does not seem to affect her orgasm potential. This is a truly remarkable finding and difficult to believe. One is reluctant to accept the message that a girl's history of sexual experience and her apparent capability of attracting and pleasing males count for nought in her later ability to achieve orgasm during regular intercourse.

The crucial question must then be asked as to whether sexual practice does materially affect orgasm consistency. This is pivotal in deciding how modifiable orgasm capacity is, once a girl's basic socialization experiences have occurred. Kinsey, *et al.* (1953), who have published the most reliable data bearing on this matter, reported that practice derived from regular married intercourse did have an appreciable effect on the likelihood of attaining at least '*occasional*' orgasm. Illustratively, while 75 per cent of married women attained at least occasional orgasm during the first year of marriage, this increased to 83 per cent by the fifth year and 89 per cent by the twentieth year. In other words, there was a 14 per cent increase in this 'at least occasional' orgasm category over a twenty-year span. Another way to look at this result is that it represents a 14 per cent decrease in those who 'never' attain orgasm. Note too that over the span of the first three months of marriage there was an analogous 10 per cent decrease in the 'never'-attain-orgasm category. But approaching the Kinsey, *et al.* data from another perspective, one finds that the percentage of women who attained orgasm in 'nearly all' (90–100 per cent) of their relations increased only 8 per cent from the first to the twentieth year of marriage. In other words, twenty years of practice produced an 8 per cent increment in those able to attain orgasm with high regularity. It is of further interest that while 39 per cent of married women attained orgasm 90 to 100 per cent of the time during their first year of marriage, this value increased to only 40 per cent by the fifth year of marriage. After five years of practice only a 1 per cent increase could be detected! Even after ten years of practice the increase was only 3 per cent. If one looks at the less extreme category of those women able to attain orgasm 60–89 per cent of the time, one finds only a 3 per cent improvement after five years of practice and a 5 per cent improvement after ten years.

The rates of improvement just cited strike me as being quite small. However, it should be acknowledged that Kinsey, *et al.* (1953) chose a different interpretative framework. They stated (p. 384): 'These data provide impressive evidence that experience and psychological reconditioning may, in the course of time, improve the ability of the female to respond to the point of orgasm in her marital coitus.' The Kinsey, *et al.* view seems exaggerated in its optimism. If after five years of practice only 1 per cent show an increase in being really consistently orgasmic, or if after five years of practice only 8 per cent of those who are *totally* nonorgasmic begin to have an occasional orgasm, how can one attribute much influence to practice effects? This role of practice is detectable but otherwise of small proportions. Overall, it is my impression that practice may, to a limited degree, decrease a woman's likelihood of *never* reaching orgasm during intercourse, but that it has minimal effect on her probability of attaining orgasm with high consistency. Intensive practice can help a woman who has serious difficulty in attaining orgasm at all to build up an orgasmic level of excitement occasionally; but it seems rarely to transform her into one who achieves orgasm with great consistency.

Incidentally, there is another factor to consider which cautions one to interpret conservatively even the small practice effects observed by Kinsey, *et al.* One must consider the possibility that with increasing duration of marriage there is greater assurance on a woman's part that her husband is a dependable love object (that he can be counted upon to remain with her); and it may be her diminished concern about his dependability, rather than practice effects, which facilitates her achievement of orgasm. Indeed, as one further scans the Kinsey, *et al.* data concerned with practice effects, other questions arise. For example, is it really logical to attribute any of the gains in orgasm consistency which may occur beyond the fifth year of marriage to practice? Would one not expect the potential maximum facilitation due to practice to have already been approached in the first five years of marriage when youthful vigour and intercourse rates are at their height? Another question that presents itself is why the apparent effect of practice should register primarily in terms of facilitation of the nonorgasmic woman to the point where she can be occasionally orgasmic? If practice is a prime factor in reaching orgasm, why does it so rarely enable a woman with low-orgasm consistency to become highly consistent? In my opinion, this last question is of paramount import and stands as an impressive objection to any theory which underscores the role of practice, as such, in shaping orgasm potential.

If one respects the information presented and the train of logic pursued, it becomes difficult to evade the conclusion that a woman's orgasm potential is probably determined by conditions relatively early in her life, well before she becomes sexually active. We know practically nothing about the specific socialization conditions which facilitate or inhibit orgasm potential. The only hint we have is that certain attitudes on father's part may be especially critical. Apparently, a woman's orgasm potential is at least partially a function of whether she was able to perceive her father as dependably interested in her. Why the mother's attitudes have not been implicated in the shaping of orgasmic potential remains a mystery. Despite an earlier attempt to cope with this puzzle by suggesting that it is, after all, logical that a mode of response to a current male love object should be particularly linked to experiences with the original prime male love object (father), it still seems strange that feelings about the original female model (mother) should not also be implicated. Of course, the present studies have dealt only with a woman's *recall* of her mother's qualities, and it is possible that if more direct study of the mothers themselves had been possible then some significant correlations between a woman's orgasm consistency and her mother's attributes would have been obtained. One can also speculate that the difficulty in detecting the influence of mother may stem from the fact that those of her attributes which are important involve not so much specific traits or qualities as her attitude towards her husband. Illustratively, if she relates to him in a way which suggests that she thinks he is a dependable person and that his love can be counted upon, this might convey to her daughter the message that not only father but also men in general can be taken as dependable love objects. Clarification of this issue would appear to be an important area for research exploration.

In originally offering a model to explain the possible influence of a woman's feelings about love object dependability upon her orgasm consistency, emphasis was placed upon the fact that the process of attaining orgasm involves a retreat from what is 'out there' induced not only by diminished sensory acuity but also by focusing upon immediate body experiences which diminish awareness of outside objects. It means, for the average woman, giving up her perceptual hold on the usual world of objects and allowing herself to be 'carried away' by sensations which are aroused in her by a man's behaviour. I earlier conjectured that if a woman has pre-existing doubts about the dependability of love objects, the process of becoming sexually excited is disturbing to her not only because it results in a less articulated perceptual 'hold' on objects in general, but also because, while in this less articulated condition, she has to 'trust' the behaviour of a man who, via his stimulating behaviour, exerts control over her state of consciousness and the clarity of her object relations. Presumably, if she finds such conditions too threatening she will develop anxiety which inhibits the build-up of sexual excitement and blocks orgasm. One cannot help wondering whether the woman with low-orgasm consistency might not also have difficulties in other situations in which the action of some outside male agent produces changes in her level of consciousness or exerts control over the way she experiences the world. For example, would she find a hypnotic induction procedure particularly threatening? Would she respond with special negativism to medical procedures which produced loss of consciousness or called for 'submission' to a physician who would be in a position to do radical things to her which she could not control?

Actually, one might expect that orgasm would be facilitated by any conditions which increase a woman's feeling that the man with whom she is having sexual intercourse can be counted on to be loyal and to maintain steadfast interest in her. What are the practical implications of this generalization? Consider some illustrative formulations or hypotheses.

1. A woman will probably be more orgasmic with a man when her relationship with him has been formally stabilized (as through marriage).

2. A woman should be less orgasmic in transient, temporary sexual liaisons.

3. Increasing duration of marriage (within certain age limits) should increase orgasm consistency.

4. Conditions which magnify the probability of a husband having to be absent unpredictably (for example, war duty, job responsibilities) should decrease the wife's orgasm consistency.

5. A wife's discovery of husband's infidelity with other women should decrease her orgasm consistency.

6. Wives who find themselves in competition with other wives (as in a polygamous culture) should manifest decreased orgasm consistency.

7. A woman whose husband cannot give up close investment in his mother, and who is therefore uncertain of his investment in her as his wife, should have special orgasm difficulties.

8. While one would be tempted to argue that the birth of a child would help to reassure a woman about the stability of her marriage and therefore to enhance her orgasm consistency, there are also other repercussions of a birth (for example, its possible estranging effect on the husband who sees the new child as a competitor), which prevent such a simple generalization. Perhaps one could say that if a child is born to a marriage and the husband is genuinely pleased by the event (does not feel seriously competitive with the child) this may, via its further formalization of the long-term nature of the marriage, increase the wife's orgasm potential.

The Clitoral-Vaginal Controversy

Rarely have there been so many opinionated assertions based on absolutely no evidence as one finds in the literature dealing with clitoral versus vaginal arousal. It was largely within psychoanalytic circles, at Freud's behest, that the myth evolved that enjoyment of vaginal stimulation by a woman is more mature or healthy than is enjoyment of direct (manual or oral) clitoral arousal. The clitoris was considered to be a phallic-like organ and preference for direct clitoral stimulation was labelled as unfeminine. Even the Masters and Johnson (1966) report that a major part of the arousal produced by movements of the penis in the vagina is achieved indirectly through clitoral stimulation has not done much to discourage the view that 'clitoral' orgasm is somehow inferior. Masters and Johnson (along with Kinsey, *et al.*) went so far as to propose that vaginal stimulation, *as such*, adds little to the total arousal elicited by intercourse. They pointed out that sensory receptors are almost absent from the vaginal wall and therefore discounted the role of sensations from the vagina in building up to orgasmic excitement. This extreme position does not appear to be justified. Women can distinguish the patterns of sensations they experience from direct vaginal versus direct clitoral stimulation; and they often have strong preferences for one or the other. While the vaginal wall may have few sensory receptors, there is no question that the kinesthetic sensations produced by penile intromission can be perceived and have highly erotic significance. One must also assume that there is major arousing significance for many women in the mere fact of being vaginally penetrated.

Our studies did clearly demonstrate that women differ considerably in the degree to which they prefer direct clitoral versus vaginal stimulation during intercourse. Some prefer only direct vaginal stimulation and even find direct clitoral arousal to be unpleasant. Others get 'nothing' out of penile intromission and extract all of their sexual excitement from direct manual manipulation of the clitoris. However, the information collected did indicate that the average woman tends to rate manual clitoral manipulation as a particularly important component of the arousal sequence and 19 per cent consider it absolutely essential for reaching orgasm. When asked to choose between having either clitoral or vaginal stimulation, 64 per cent gave their vote to clitoral. Thirty per cent of women in one sample indicated that even while penile intromission is occurring they require the final assistance of direct clitoral manipulation in order to reach their orgasm threshold. There is no question that the average woman finds direct manual clitoral manipulation a sizeable component of the stimulation needed to reach orgasm.

The woman who prefers manual clitoral stimulation does not differ in her orgasm consistency from the one preferring vaginal modes of arousal. Either form of stimulation is just as effective as the other when judged in terms of orgasm attainment. It is also extremely important, in view of past speculations that vaginally focused stimulation produces a 'better' orgasm, to add that I found no correlations which would favour such a conclusion. Actually, if there is a 'better' species of orgasm linked with one or the other mode of stimulation, the findings favour the direct clitoral species. I actually detected a trend for women with high clitoral preference to exceed those with high vaginal preference in the degree to which they experience orgasm as being of 'ecstatic' intensity. Apparently, the clitorally oriented woman experiences a higher charge of whatever is encompassed by the term 'ecstatic' than does the vaginally oriented woman. This difference eventually turned out to be congruent with other data analyses which suggested that there might be a basic difference in the clitoral versus vaginally oriented with respect to the way they modulate arousal or excitement. Early in my studies an important differentiation between the clitorally and vaginally oriented was detected with respect to how they experience their bodies. Fairly convincing evidence was obtained that the greater a woman's vaginal orientation the more likely she is to report that her body feels 'distant', 'not mine', and diminished in sensitivity. The more vaginally oriented woman seemed to perceive her body as lacking vitality, sensitivity, and the quality of vividness or aliveness that one's own body customarily has.

Analogous to this finding, other results I obtained indicated that the more vaginally oriented woman is inclined to 'dampen' excitement and to minimize the potentially arousing aspects of what she perceives. When constructing imaginative stories she minimizes and mutes tension or crisis. Problems within her stories are resolved in a 'they lived happily ever after' fashion. While casting about for an explanation as to why the vaginally oriented woman is inclined to mute experience, a logical possibility presented itself in terms of the finding that she is more anxious than the clitorally oriented. As defined by several different measures, amount of anxiety was observed to be positively linked with strength of vaginal preference. This suggested that the muting of both body and nonbody stimuli by the vaginally oriented might be a defence against anxiety. They might learn to dampen the intensity of what they experience in an attempt to evade the chronic unpleasant sensations associated with anxiety.

I would caution that although the vaginally oriented have been described as more anxious than the clitorally oriented, this in no way is meant to imply that they are less 'healthy' or that they are seriously maladjusted. There is no intent to replace the equation between vaginal response and maturity which has so long been common in the psychoanalytic literature with a reverse equation. The women who were studied were without gross psychiatric symptomatology and generally functioned at what would be considered a 'normal' level. There is no justification for labelling the vaginally oriented women as really disturbed or maladjusted.

It should be added that the fact that the vaginally oriented woman is more anxious or has experienced more psychological distress than the clitorally oriented does not mean that she is less mature or that she is somehow psychologically inferior. The women with these differing orientations may simply differ in how their tension shows itself when they run into difficulties. For example, those with a clitoral preference may channel their disturbance into preoccupation with minor body complaints or defensive compulsiveness rather than anxious distress.

I earlier proposed several possible hypotheses to explain why a vaginal orientation should be linked with the 'muting' style of coping with stimuli. Briefly they were as follows:

1. Vaginal stimulation may generally produce less intense excitement than manual clitoral stimulation and therefore be less threatening to a woman who wants to keep her experiences muted or subdued.

2. The vaginally oriented woman's depersonalized way of experiencing her body might make her relatively unresponsive to sexual stimulation unless it was delivered in a way that had unusually intense *psychological* connotations. The specific act of intercourse, with its special significance of intimacy, might be necessary to get through the coldness or unresponsiveness possibly associated with a depersonalized set. Perhaps direct clitoral stimulation lacks the *personalized* psychological intensity produced by penile penetration and cannot overcome a depersonalized body set.

3. Another possibility is that the vaginally oriented woman who, as shown by my findings, has a tendency to recall her father as not having been willing to respond *positively* to her, needs an extra commitment from a man, in the form of penile penetration, before she is willing to respond to him.

4. Finally, the possibility was considered that the vaginally oriented woman, because of her depersonalized way of experiencing her body, may have an unusually hazy concept of her genital area and so require the active articulation of the vaginal space by the penis in order to be able to 'tune in' on sensation in the genital region in a focused fashion.

When I scanned the empirical differences which we found between the vaginally and clitorally oriented, I was particularly impressed with the potential explanatory value of the fact that there was a greater sense of body Depersonalization in the former group. The vaginally oriented woman indicated with fair consistency that she felt estranged and distant from her body, as if it did not belong to her personally. The possible utility of such depersonalization in defending against anxiety has already been discussed. There were also some other possible implications which came to mind. A depersonalized feeling about one's body might be a way of denying responsibility for what happens to, or is experienced via, the body. It could be a means of denying responsibility for the general realm of body events. In other words, depersonalization might represent a rejection of the somatic dimensions of self. What might motivate a woman to do this? One possibility would be that she grew up in a highly puritanical family in which the body was portrayed as a bad object, a source of evil. Depersonalization would be a way of denying ownership of the bad object. However, this does not seem to be a likely explanation in view of the fact that clitoral-vaginal preference was found to be uncorrelated with any of the measures of religiosity and formal church behaviour which were employed and which one would expect to be linked with puritanical socialization.

Another alternative which was pondered is that the Depersonalized attitude might be a way of stealing the self against anticipated attack upon, or exploitation of, one's body. A woman who expects that her body will be the target of great hostility or that it will be misused in some way might want to disown it, not as a bad object but rather as one that will incur unpleasantness. It is as if she felt, 'I am certain my body is going to get hurt or be exploited, so I want to be as little associated with it as possible.' Such an attitude might possibly be instilled by having to endure long periods of illness in oneself or in some important family member. It could derive too from a sado-masochistic concept of femaleness, especially its sexual aspects. There might be a vivid belief that sexual intercourse is painful and involves potential body damage and danger. The male sex partner would be visualized as destructive and exploiting. There is little in the way of empirical data either to affirm or reject this possibility. If it were to turn out to be reasonable, it might have implications for the vaginal versus clitoral preference. Perhaps a woman who visualizes sexual stimulation as being inextricably linked with a situation in which a man aggresses against her by literally penetrating her body cannot build up sexual excitement unless the act of penetration occurs. It may be necessary for her to know that she is penetrated and thus to give the sex partner's approach to her some potential meaning of 'forcible entry' or body exploitation before she can assimilate stimulation as being really sexual.

These were some of the possibilities and speculations which I entertained when considering the significance of the findings relating to depersonalization. However, none of these hypotheses could be affirmed or disaffirmed on the basis of the actual empirical findings available. Furthermore, none offered clarification as to why the clitorally oriented woman does not enjoy vaginal stimulation.

To seek additional clarification, another line of analysis was undertaken which involved considering in more detail the exact nature of what clitoral and vaginal stimulation mean. If one accepts the observations of Kinsey, *et al.* (1953) and Masters and Johnson (1966), it would have to be agreed that penile intromission delivers a large amount of stimulation to the clitoris. The vaginally oriented woman does receive a substantial quantity of clitoral stimulation. However, this occurs indirectly. The stimulation is delivered by the penis (by traction exerted on the wings of the clitoral hood), rather than by direct manual manipulation. Relatedly, direct manual arousal of the clitoris produces vaginal excitation and pulsation and, as excitement builds up, a variety of kinesthetic sensations in the pelvic musculature which may be analogous to some of the sensations induced by penile penetration. Clearly, there are common elements in the two forms of sexual stimulation. One would have to say that the vaginally oriented woman experiences many of the arousal elements that are basic to the clitoral orientation, and likewise one would have to agree that the clitorally oriented woman builds her excitement on sensations and cues which are not dissimilar from those utilized by the vaginally oriented. Whether a woman is clitoral or vaginal in preference, she does receive stimulation of the clitoris; does experience vaginal changes and pulsations; and does become aware of a muscle tension build up, with accompanying intense kinesthetic sensations. One should add that the overlap between the clitoral and vaginal orientations is further fostered by the fact that a majority of persons engaging in sexual relationships use both direct clitoral and also vaginal stimulation successively and simultaneously, resulting in a complex blend of the two. Even psychologically the clitorally and vaginally oriented experience much in common. In both instances, there is typically an interaction with a man who is sexually aroused and who is interested in eliciting as much excitement or response as possible.

What then, is the nature of the experiential distinction which the clitorally oriented – as compared to the vaginally oriented – woman is reacting to during sexual interaction? Obviously, this distinction relates primarily to the fact that in one case the stimulation that is most preferred is delivered by the penis while inserted in the vagina, and in the other case the preferred stimulation is manually (orally) delivered to the clitoral region. Penile intromission is particularly valued in the one instance, while manual stroking of the clitoris seems primary in the other instance. The problem of explaining vaginal versus clitoral orientation becomes one of clarifying the differential significance of the male sex partner inserting his penis into the vagina as compared to his using his hand to stimulate the clitoris.

Can one not conceptualize this difference in terms of role differences? The woman who is receiving stimulation from a man who has his penis inserted in her vagina is engaged in an act of *mutual* stimulation At the same time that the man is trying to bring her to orgasm she is doing likewise for him. It is a transaction in which they are both closely and equally involved. This contrasts with the situation in which manual clitoral stimulation is applied by a man. In this instance the woman is receiving stimulation intended to arouse her to orgasm; and while the man may also be receiving arousing stimulation from her, it is usually not immediately intended to produce orgasm, as such. She occupies the role of the principal receiver. His is the relatively more detached role. He will have either already attained orgasm or will do so after she has reached orgasm. What this means is that the vaginally oriented woman is stimulated to orgasm during a transaction in which the sex partner is equally involved as a giver and taker. The clitorally oriented woman is aroused to orgasm in a context where she is the primary receiver and her sex partner is in many respects a spectator or onlooker. If this analysis is correct, it means that the greater a woman's clitoral orientation the more she prefers achieving orgasmic excitement in a context in which she is the central object, in which her partner is clearly separate and largely giving his attention to her. The vaginally oriented woman could be said to prefer that her orgasmic excitement be generated in an interchange in which she is not the observed object, but rather 'fused' with a partner who is as equally involved as she is.

Related to this formulation is another obvious difference between the conditions of vaginal versus direct clitoral stimulation. In the first instance the primary aspect of the sexual transaction involves vaginal penetration and a resultant unique closeness of two bodies. In the second instance the bodies of the two sex partners are more clearly separate. On this basis, too, one can say that delivery of manual clitoral stimulation leaves the male sex partner relatively more psychologically detached than does delivery of vaginal stimulation. There is great intimacy in both contexts, but there are differences in the degree to which the woman can think of herself as a 'separate' entity. How do such formulations relate to other differences between the clitorally and vaginally oriented which have appeared in our data? They immediately seem to lead right back to the greater tendency of the vaginally oriented woman to experience her body as depersonalized. The essence of the depersonalized feeling is that one's body is alien, distant, and not truly a part of self. In other words, there is a sense of not having full ownership of one's own body. This may represent a belief on the part of the vaginally oriented woman that she has no right to feel that her body belongs to herself or to enjoy body experiences that only gratify her personally. She might, then, further believe that an intense body experience like sexual arousal should occur only when someone else, a male sex partner, becomes so closely involved with her body that he is sharing in the responsibility for it. In other words, when her body is fused sexually with his, she can think of her sexual arousal as a joint event. She can perceive the experiences as not primarily for her own satisfaction but also for another. At the other extreme, the clitorally oriented woman would, from this viewpoint, have the opposing need to experience her body autonomously and to be reassured that an event like intense sexual excitement belonged clearly and personally to her. She would be a person who would have a negative response to conditions which seriously challenged her sense of body autonomy.

How might such attitudinal differences between the vaginally and clitorally oriented with respect to the autonomy of one's body arise? There is no solid information available upon which to construct an answer. One can only speculate that parental attitudes play a prime role. The vaginally oriented woman could be pictured as having grown up in a family in which she was made to feel that she was obligated to her parents and had only limited rights to enjoy anything unless they approved or could derive indirect profit from it themselves. That is, she would be made to feel that her parents had important proprietary rights over her – and her body. The sense of not having body autonomy might be particularly fostered if the parents promulgated strict rules about various kinds of body activities. For example, if they emphasized that she could use her body for sexual purposes only under special conditions which they would spell out, they would be giving her the message that, in this realm, her body really was only partially under her own control. They would, in essence, be telling her that an important aspect of her body functioning was alienated from her own decision-making. It is possible that similar feelings of not being in possession of one's body could be encouraged by parents who demanded strict adherence to certain standards about eating or who enforced elaborate arbitrary rituals with regard to toilet training. The basic attitude would be shaped that one dare not have a really important or dramatic body experience unless it was approved by, or shared with, some other significant figure.

What can one say about the possible socialization background of the clitorally oriented woman? It is quite conceivable that she too grew up with parents who made the same demands for proprietary rights over her body as have been speculatively attributed to the parents of the vaginally oriented. However, instead of acquiescing to these demands, she may have rejected them and adopted compensatory defences built around the idea that she would not permit intrusion upon the autonomy of her body. This would mean that she would be wary of situations in which her perception of her body as a clearly separate entity might be violated. One can also conceive of such an orientation being encouraged in a family setting in which there was an exaggerated, and probably defensive emphasis placed on being autonomous and not allowing one's individuality to be encroached upon by others. It will be a difficult task to test this formulation empirically. There might be multiple patterns of parent behaviour which would encourage either a loss of sense of body ownership or an opposite exaggerated feeling of body autonomy. Such attitudes could be a function of parents' moralistic expectations about sex or their special ideas about eating and adoption of their perfectionistic demands for control of anal functions and maintenance of body cleanliness. One can think of manifold other possibilities – also, for example, the parental assumption that the child's body has to be carefully watched and controlled in order to protect it from accidents or other physical trauma. The various ways in which parental control over the body might be exercised would make it difficult to specify a particular parental attribute which would be predictive of a daughter adopting a clitoral versus vaginal orientation.

The entire question of clitoral versus vaginal preference is obviously extremely complex. Only a small beginning has been made in understanding its psychological components.

Sexual Appetite

One of the questions which I explored throughout our studies concerns the relationship of sexual appetite to other forms of appetite. Does the woman who has high orgasm consistency or who has a high intercourse rate show special gusto with reference to other gratifications? Many other forms of 'appetite' have been appraised. Measures were taken of satisfaction derived from eating and the range of foods enjoyed. Information was obtained too about consumption of alcohol and cigarette smoking. Determinations were made of amount of enjoyment of athletics and of the use of the large muscles of the body. Systematic inquiry was undertaken about how much new experience and novelty (and the accompanying excitement) were sought after. There were also measures of amount of time spent per week in seeking entertainment (for example, watching TV), amount of effort devoted to narcissistically oriented self-grooming activities, and preferences for visual versus kinesthetic experiences. An analysis of the data emanating from these diverse measures has failed to establish more than a few isolated links between sexual appetite and other forms of appetite. The 'sexy' woman is not likely to enjoy food more than the less 'sexy' one. She is also not more likely to enjoy alcohol or smoking or athletic activities. Sexual appetite cannot be easily conceptualized as a manifestation of a more generalized zest for gratification. It is important to add that the data have not even hinted at a *compensatory* relationship between the area of sexual gratification and other modes of gratification. That is, there is no sign that the woman who has difficulty in reaching orgasm or who feels unsatisfied after orgasm is inclined, by way of compensation, to be unusually interested in food. Nor is she unusually interested in alcohol or smoking. If inability to attain sexual satisfaction does result in compensatory forms of behaviour they lie outside of the wide area which was studied. It is pertinent that one cannot even say (in terms of the data collected) that lack of satisfaction from sexual interaction raises amount of tension, insofar as it is detectable in the form of anxiety or hostile irritability or achievement fantasies or even general body awareness. Such findings, if affirmed by further studies, would seem to have considerable relevance for theories which view sexual tension in the context of a hydraulic system – i.e., that if the tension does not find an outlet in one sector, it will increase the pressure in another.

My findings would suggest, on the contrary, that within the range of sexual gratification characterizing the married women who were studied, there was adaptation to the level of satisfaction available. There were no indications that women with very low orgasm rates were more tense or irritable or more interested in other appetites like eating than women with high orgasm rates.

This is a fairly radical conclusion, but congruent with the facts. It must be cautioned that one cannot validly apply such a perspective to women who almost totally lack opportunity for heterosexual intimacy. Perhaps there are certain minimum quantities of sexual contact which are necessary to prevent the build-up of disturbing tension. While there would probably be individual differences in this area, one wonders whether the average woman might not quite successfully adapt to rates of sexual interaction considerably below current averages for married women.

With respect to the matter of the effects associated with different quantities of sexual contact, we do not know such simple things as whether there are changes in tension levels of women as they shift from the state of limited sexual contact usually typifying the unmarried role to the state of considerable sexual contact accompanying marriage. We do not know whether the shift results in increasing or decreasing other areas of appetite. We do not know in what ways a woman feels different after intercourse producing orgasm against intercourse which does not eventuate in orgasm. If there are differences, are they transitory or do they last for long periods? In a related vein, we do not know whether a woman who usually fails to attain orgasm learns to focus in a compensatory fashion upon other aspects of the sexual experience. Perhaps she begins to 'tune in' more to the sheer intimacy of each sexual contact or the skin sensations it creates or to the 'feel' of being penetrated. Conceivably, she might even begin to develop a special 'taste' for the quality of heightened tension which is never directly or grossly relieved. She might learn to enjoy her own more gradual strategies (both during and after intercourse) for dissipating her sexual arousal.

The question of how much sexual contact a woman 'needs' leads logically to the matter of intercourse frequency. As earlier reported, other investigators and I have found enormous differences in women's intercourse rates. While there is little doubt that husband's preferences are important determiners of such differences in rates, our studies suggest that another significant factor is a woman's interest in narcissistic gratification. Evidence was found that the greater a woman's intercourse rate the more energy she invests in body-enhancing procedures (for example, buying new clothes, grooming, applying cosmetics) and the more she seeks out activities which will 'entertain' her. In addition, the women with higher intercourse rates were discovered to be inclined towards exhibitionism, to prefer situations in which they are the centre of attention. These findings intimated that one of the elements motivating higher intercourse rates is a need for large amounts of attention. The intercourse situation is one in which a woman may find not only sexual stimulation but also the close attention of another who communicates admiration and lavishes interest on her body.

The fact that narcissistic and exhibitionistic wishes seem to play a part in intercourse frequency raises the more general issue of what are the major components of gratification that the average woman seeks in a sexual contact. What is the weight that she assigns to sexual arousal, as such, as compared to variables like an opportunity for intimacy or interaction with a man who invests his attention in her? We do not have scientific information which would even begin to clarify this matter. It is a safe guess, though, that one would probably find that individual women differ considerably as to which components of intercourse they most value. Further, one would conjecture that at different stages of her life a woman might change with respect to the component that was most important to her. Sexual arousal might be the most prominent element in the early stage of marriage; intimacy might become particularly important following the death of some important figure (for example, a parent); and narcissistic gratification derived from being the focus of the partner's attention might gain ascendancy after events signifying failure or loss of self-esteem. It is well to keep in mind the potential diversity of the psychological elements associated with intercourse which may appeal to a woman. In addition to those mentioned above, one might, by way of illustration, enumerate the following ways in which a woman could utilize intercourse:

To reassure herself of her femininity
To dispel her boredom
To gain power over her sex partner

To affirm her attractiveness
To obtain unusual or even painful sensory experiences
To find release from her own usually over-rigid self control
To be held and comforted

Returning to the eating analogy earlier cited, it would come as no surprise if one stated that people eat not only to gratify hunger but also diversely because they enjoy the taste, find the social interactions during meals to be gratifying, like the range of sensory experiences they obtain, and find that the routine of eating is an interesting ritual which often relieves boredom.

Masturbation

One form of sexual gratification I found to be very little utilized by the married women in the various samples was masturbation. The average woman said she masturbates 'rarely'. Relatedly, Kinsey, *et al* (1953) found masturbation (to orgasm) to occur, on the average, about once or twice a month in married women. Nevertheless, it is of interest that married women masturbate at all, in view of the fact that they have regular intercourse available. While some of such mastubatory behaviour might be attributed to factors like the wish for sexual stimulation when the husband is absent from home (for example, away on a business trip), there are suggestions that other factors too play a role. It will be recalled that our findings indicated that the woman who is least likely to masturbate and who says she least enjoys it is characterized by certain attributes. There was evidence that the more a woman refrains from masturbation the more she is opposed to greater freedom in sexual matters; the less explicitly she acknowledges the importance of sex in her life; the more she prefers a routine that is orderly, systematic, and not messy (unclean); the more she expresses belief in the existence of God and in religious ideals (but is not more religious, as defined by formal religious behaviour like church attendance); the more she recalls her mother as having been moralistically strict; and the less she recalls her mother as having been distant, unloving, and neglecting. When the last finding pertaining to the mother was originally interpreted, emphasis was placed on the fact that this was the first instance in which a measure of sexual behaviour was significantly linked with attitudes toward mother rather than father. In view of the fact that those most inclined to masturbate perceived their mothers as rejecting and unloving, it was proposed that masturbation might be a way of asserting the independence of one's body from mother, a declaration of freedom from her and an assertion of ability to be separate from her. The underlying note of defiance in masturbation is implied too in the fact that amount of masturbation was found to be positively correlated with declarations that there should be more sexual freedom in our culture and with the rejections of orderly, clean, regulated ways of doing things. There does seem to be a note of self-assertion in the attitude of the woman who is inclined towards masturbation. At the same time, it must be cautioned that there is no evidence that she is *generally* hostile or aggressive or antagonistic to an unusual degree. Her defiance seems to be confined to limited sectors of attitude and behaviour. One might almost say that she finds it sufficiently expressive of her defiance to engage periodically in masturbation. The association of masturbation with that which is bad, messy, and immoral needs to be reiterated. Apparently, one of the factors which inhibits masturbation is that it is perceived both figuratively and literally as a 'dirty' thing. As earlier noted, this is the only aspect of sexual behaviour which I found to be related to attitudes about being dirty. It is also the only aspect found to be linked with certain aspects of religiosity. Interestingly, Kinsey, *et al.* (1953) also found the amount of masturbatory behaviour to be clearly lower in the religiously devout than nondevout. But they found few, if any, relationships between religiosity and other aspects of sex behaviour (except homosexuality and premarital sex contacts). A similar lack of relationship between religiosity and most aspects of sexual behaviour has characterized our data.

Multiple factors contribute to a woman's motivation to masturbate. Kinsey, *et al.* (1953) have shown that she will turn to masturbation when other forms of sexual gratification are not available. Our data indicate, in addition, that she may turn to masturbation as a way of expressing independence and defiance. At the same time, impulses to masturbate growing out of such motivations must overcome inhibitory feelings which define masturbation as dirty and immoral. The amount of masturbation probably represents, then, in each individual case, a unique balance among the factors cited which both positively motivate and also inhibit masturbatory interest. Another point that needs to be reiterated is that masturbation in married women does not appear to be a compensation for deficiencies in other aspects of sexual behaviour. Masturbation frequency turned out not to be related to orgasm consistency. It was also unrelated to preferred and actual intercourse frequencies, strength of orgasm, amount of satisfaction derived from orgasm, and many other indices concerned with sexual responsiveness. One cannot justifiedly think of the woman who masturbates with relatively high frequency (at least if she is not too extremely beyond the range found in samples of normal married women) as trying to obtain substitute gratification for failure in sexual intercourse encounters. Masturbatory behaviour, as it was reported in the various samples studied, is also unrelated to anxiety level or other measures having to do with one's 'mental health'. There is no support for considering masturbation, in any general sense, a sign of disturbing psychological tensions. This does not rule out the possibility that some individual woman might utilize masturbation as a channel for releasing disturbing affect or acting out conflict wishes, but, of course, any segment of behaviour can be adapted to such ends.

Little is known about how married women define their masturbatory activity within the context of their marriage relationship. We do not have data about whether they keep their masturbation secret from their husbands. Do they ever masturbate in the husband's presence? Do they discuss masturbation with their husbands as freely as they discuss other aspects of sexuality? Such information would provide a more accurate basis for evaluating the role of masturbation in the average woman's life. If one had to guess, it is probably likely that most wives conceal their masturbation and rarely talk openly about it. They are probably reluctant to discuss it with their husbands, not only because of its 'dirty' connotations, but also because it could easily be interpreted as depreciatory of the husband's sexual prowess. One negative result with respect to the masturbation findings deserves special comment. I discovered that neither masturbation frequency nor amount of satisfaction from masturbation was significantly related to clitoral-vaginal preference. There was not even a hint of a relationship. One might have expected that the clitorally oriented woman who particularly enjoys manual manipulation (which is usually focused in the clitoral area) would also have a special liking for masturbation, which is also manual in character, and in most instances directed to the vicinity of the clitoris (Kinsey, *et al.*, 1953). The fact that this expectation was not fulfilled suggests that the two modes of excitation, although involving analogous anatomical areas, are quite different psychologically. But is this true?

It was proposed earlier that what is typical of the clitorally oriented woman is that she prefers a sexual context in which she can feel that she has full possession of her own body, that it is not fused with the body of another. If so, would not the masturbatory situation, which does not involve a sex partner at all, be an even clearer instance of what the clitorally oriented woman prefers? Does this not imply a considerable similarity between the two forms of sexual stimulation? Perhaps so, but the similarity may be only superficial. First of all, there is evidence that while the clitorally oriented woman wants to maintain a sense of being in full possession of her own body, one of the motivations for masturbation is to express a defiant independence (of mother). That is, masturbation goes a step beyond the simple assertion of self-ownership to a more defiant rejection of any outside hold on one's body. Masturbation may represent psychologically a more radical position with respect to how one wants one's body to be related to others (at a sexual level) than the clitorally oriented woman seeks.

Laing (1959) and others have pointed out another aspect of masturbation which may differentiate it psychologically from the needs of the clitorally oriented woman. In analysing the act of masturbation they have been impressed with how often it takes on an unreal quality and involves relating to a fantasied or imaginary partner. That is, in the process of masturbating there is an isolation from others and a deviation from accepted norms which imparts to it an unusual aura of unreality. Laing states (p. 40): 'The awareness the masturbator has of his body is complicated by the fact that his body has been seduced from real action into participation in an imaginary situation.' He adds, 'The body as used in the act of masturbation is employed with the express intention of gaining satisfaction by eliminating the problems of coping with other real bodies . . . The "real" other person who is the object of desire becomes merely the shadow of the imagined other. This is one of the problems the masturbator runs into: his imagination casts its shadow over him . . .' One of the implications of this view is that during masturbation a woman would find that her body takes on somewhat strange, unreal qualities; and in that sense might seem to belong less to herself than it usually does. Relatedly, Laing and other (in Masters [ed.], 1967) have also remarked that during masturbation the individual is forced to take several divided perspectives toward his own body. He is simultaneously the recipient of stimulation, the giver of stimulation, and perhaps in fantasy still another figure who has been brought into the act. This could mean that masturbation encourages a division of identity and also multiple modes of regarding or experiencing one's own body. The clitorally oriented woman, who has been speculatively portrayed as motivated to maintain a clear sense of 'my body belongs to me', might find the unreality of the masturbatory situation and its encouragement of multiple modes of experiencing one's body to be unacceptable. What about the vaginally oriented woman? One would presume that while the sharing of her body with others, which she could achieve through fantasy during masturbation, might please her, she would find the literal isolation of her body (and the obvious fact that its experiences would be her sole responsibility) to be unpleasant.

A matter of special interest with regard to masturbation derives from the Kinsey, *et al.* (1953) observation that of the 62 per cent of their total sample of women who reported ever having masturbated, only 4 to 6 per cent did not attain orgasm. That is, about 96 per cent of these women would reach orgasm via their self-stimulation. The 4 to 6 per cent who could not may be contrasted with the considerably higher percentages who fail to achieve orgasm while stimulated by a male sex partner. Even after five years of marriage 17 per cent of married women have not had an orgasm during their sexual contacts with their husbands. One possible explanation of this difference might be that the 68 per cent of women who do report masturbating represent a special selective sample with unusual orgasmic potential and that their superiority in this respect would also be evidenced in their sexual response to a male partner. That is, only 4 to 6 per cent of them would be completely nonorgasmic with a sex partner. However, this is unlikely for two reasons. First, I found in the samples we studied that frequency of masturbation had only a chance relationship to orgasm consistency. Furthermore, in the Kinsey, *et al.* data one finds that even of those women with considerable masturbatory experience prior to marriage, 16 per cent still achieved no orgasms at all during the first year of marriage. This 16 per cent clearly exceeds the 4 to 6 per cent who cannot achieve orgasm via masturbation. There is no obvious, simple way to dismiss the apparently greater ability of women to attain orgasm during masturbation than in interaction with a male sex partner. One must conclude that the presence of the male sex partner introduces an antiorgasm influence. Is this antiorgasm influence merely due to the poorer stimulation techniques of the male as compared to those which a woman can bring to bear on her own body? That is, are women simply more skilful in how they apply stimulation to their own genital areas? While this may be true in some cases, it is doubtful that it is generally true. One notes, for example, that even among extremely well-educated women, who would presumably have husbands who are well-educated (and also highly intelligent), 15 per cent fail (Kinsey, *et al.*, 1953) to attain orgasm at all after five years of marriage. One would be sceptical that the majority of husbands of such educational (and intellectual) attainment would have neglected during a five-year time span to learn a good deal about stimulating their wives. It is unlikely (although admittedly debatable) that failure to reach orgasm in such a sample would, in any major way, be due to lack of technique on the husband's part.

There is probably more logic in attributing the male sex partner's antiorgasm effect to his psychological impact. In view of my findings that inhibition of orgasm in women is correlated with fear of loss of objects one can even specifically suggest that the male partner's negative effect is due to the concern he arouses about such loss. In many cases the presence of the male sex partner appears to increase concern about object loss beyond the level which is present when a woman stimulates herself sexually. Although certain difficulties related to role and feelings of unreality were mentioned above as possibly arising during a woman's sexual self-stimulation, they seem to have less orgasm-inhibiting power than does the presence of the male sex partner. One could say that she finds *herself* a more dependable object to which to relate than she does a man. It is pertinent to this matter that Kinsey, *et al.* (1953) found that women with extensive homosexual experiences produce higher orgasm rates in their female sex partners than do men in their female sex partners after five years of marriage. Since in this homosexual instance and in that of self-stimulation the person delivering the stimulation is female, the question arises whether the orgasm-inhibiting effect of the male is somehow due to his being of a different sex. Kinsey, *et al.* specifically propose that a female may be more capable than a male of stimulating a female adequately because she has a better understanding of the feelings, sensations, and anatomy involved – and therefore has better stimulation techniques. They state (pp. 467–8):

> The higher frequency of orgasm in the homosexual contacts may have depended in part upon the considerable psychologic stimulation provided by such relationships, but there is reason for believing that it may also have depended upon the fact that two individuals of the same sex are likely to understand the anatomy and physiologic responses and psychology of their own sex better than they understand that of the opposite sex.

We have already given reasons why explanations of orgasm differences in terms of 'technique' seem inadequate. One is left with the obvious alternative of having to ask whether the process of interacting with a male figure sexually does not itself have a negative impact upon a wide range of women. This recalls the indication in our data that orgasm consistency is related to certain attitudes toward the father, but not toward mother. It may be that socialization experiences in our culture engender in a majority of women certain negative feelings toward the father which later cause them to respond in specifically negative ways (among, of course, other positive ways) to the *intimate* presence of any masculine figure. One must underscore that this entire discussion has been concerned with the negative impact of the masculine presence upon orgasm. It goes without saying, of course, that unique positive feelings and satisfactions are probably derived from sexual intimacy with a male partner; and it is unlikely that either masturbation or homosexual stimulation (in the present cultural climate) provide these satisfactions.

Psychoanalytic Theory

Most of the major theories concerning the psychological factors in sexual behaviour are directly or indirectly of psychoanalytic origin. Psychoanalysts like Freud, Ferenczi, Fenichel, and Hitschmann have attributed women's problems in sexual responsiveness primarily to variables like Oedipal conflict, guilt, fear of body damage (resulting, for example, from penetration or pregnancy), and fixation at immature psychosexual levels. How have such concepts fared in the light of the empirical information that has become available? Quite generally, one can say that a reasonable amount of support may be found for the general psychoanalytic view that difficulties in sexual response are due, at least in part, to psychological factors. Certainly, our findings pertaining to concern about object loss in orgasm consistency are congruent with such a view. Some of the observations of Kinsey, *et al.* (1953) which implicate social class and educational level in orgasm attainment are indirectly supportive of the view insofar as they make clear that a woman's sexual responsiveness is tied to her social history. The indications in our data of a correlation between orgasm potential and attitudes towards the father also analogously reinforce the general psychoanalytic position. Actually, my earlier reasoned out conclusion that orgasm potential is probably shaped by socialization experiences relatively early in a girl's life fits well with the psychoanalytic perspective.

While the empirical findings support psychoanalytic theory in its *general* emphasis on the importance of early socialization influences, they rarely fit with more specific psychoanalytic formulations. One of the first major disparities that should be mentioned involves the analytic notion that sexual responsiveness is a fundamental indicator of psychological maturity and 'mental health'. The analytic view is that psychosexual maturity is reflected in the ability to attain orgasm and even more specifically in the ability to have a so-called 'vaginal orgasm'. The vaginal orgasm has been treated in the analytic literature as one of the prime signs of whether a woman is truly mature and possessed of a sound ego structure. It has already been pointed out in several contexts that the real facts are otherwise. A woman's orgasm consistency is not linked with how psychologically immature or disturbed she is. As for the 'vaginal' orgasm, not only is there now considerable scepticism that such a species really exists in pure form, but also there is evidence that preference for vaginal as compared to clitoral stimulation is linked with variables (for example, depersonalized body attitudes, elevated anxiety) which would hardly be classified as indicative of superior ego strength.

Another major analytic proposition asserts that a woman's difficulties in reaching orgasm stem from her inability to resolve her Oedipal conflicts. Presumably, the nonorgasmic woman experiences her current sexual relationship in distorted, anxiety-provoking, guilt-evocative terms which derive from the fact that she equates it with her original Oedipal involvement with her father (and the jealous, competitive mother). It is difficult to judge in a straightforward way whether the empirical findings support such a formulation. One of the problems in rendering a judgement is the simple fact that there are many combinations of Oedipal elements and even more complex permutations as to how they may be potentially expressed. For example, Oedipal difficulties with the father may theoretically be expressed in both overattachment and unusual hostility toward him. Things are similarly complicated with respect to how Oedipal difficulties with the mother are supposedly manifested. Since I found evidence that orgasm consistency with the current sex partner is related to attitudes toward the father, one could argue that the Oedipal formulation has gained some support, insofar as a tie between feelings toward father and behaviour with respect to a contemporary sex object was affirmed. However, since feelings about the mother are also a basic component of the Oedipal dilemma and since I detected no correlations between orgasm consistency and attitudes towards mother, one could argue that the findings, at this level, do not support the overall model about how Oedipal factors inhibit sexual responsiveness. The truth is that one will have difficulty in arriving at any clear-cut decisions with respect to this matter until more precise hypotheses can be extracted concerning the relationship of sexual behaviour to the manner in which the father and mother are perceived.

Another factor often mentioned in the psychoanalytic literature as important in inhibiting a woman's orgasm potential is fear of being penetrated. It is said that anxiety about the consequences of the penis entering her body not infrequently prevents a woman from becoming sexually aroused during intercourse. Presumably the penetrating penis stirs up fantasies about internal injury, potential body damage consequent to becoming pregnant, and so forth. Relatedly, it has often been said in the analytic literature that most women envy the penis; and this envy may evoke competitive fantasies which, when intensified by sexual interactions, interfere with loving and being loved, and thus prevent orgasmic levels of excitement. No support has been found in the empirical data for either of the two formulations just outlined. Several measures of body anxiety and concern about body vulnerability proved to have only chance correlations with orgasm consistency. Also, a number of indices were utilized which indicated no relationships of consequence between orgasm consistency and attitudes with regard to male-female competition.

In general, one would have to declare that psychoanalytic concepts about sexual responsiveness in women have been largely unsupported by the available empirical evidence.

The Feminine Image

Certain psychological qualities have traditionally accompanied being a woman in Western culture. They cohere around several themes: interest in close interpersonal involvement with others; nurturant orientation; relative lack of investment in hostile and aggressive modes; delaying final role structuring until marriage; close identification of one's body with prime life goals; relative feelings of inhibition about mobility in space. What has emerged surprisingly from our data is that orgasm consistency and other measures of sexual responsiveness are not much related to whether a woman fits the feminine image as defined by such themes. Aggressive women seem to be just as sexually responsive as the non-aggressive. There are similarly no apparent differences in ability to attain sexual arousal in those low versus high in nurturance, sociability, body security, and sheer femininity of interests. One must conclude that sexual responsiveness is not *generally* a function of how well a woman conforms to the usual definition of the feminine life style. I employed a number of techniques to find out the degree to which the women in the samples studied reject conventional femininity and are actually interested in emulating masculine values. Questionnaires were administered which evaluated the amount of satisfaction with the feminine role, acceptance of established definitions of the woman's place in the family, and so forth. The data derived from these questionnaires had no consistent or generalized relationships with the indices of sex responsiveness. A woman can be in revolt against the societal definition of femininity and still be highly responsive sexually. The woman who fits the feminine model perfectly may be seriously lacking in her ability to become sexually aroused. Those qualities which figure most perceptibly in a woman's ability to enjoy sexual stimulation seem not so much to be linked to definitions of femininity as anchored in broader attitudes that cut across sex classification. Factors like concern about loss of objects, feelings of body depersonalization, religiosity, and amount of faith in the father are important in the psychological makeup of any human being, regardless of sex. It is difficult to think of a single measure specifically tapping an aspect of femininity which was consistently correlated with measures of sexual responsiveness.

This point is pertinent to other formulations which have indirectly tied sexual responsiveness to femininity via the functioning of the reproductive system. It has been popular to theorize that the woman who is adequate sexually will experience a minimum of difficulties in those physiological systems which concern reproduction and define her structurally as a woman. Presumably, the sexually adequate woman would have relatively few menstrual symptoms; would easily conceive; would have a minimum of pregnancy complications; and so forth. Such theorizing proceeds explicitly or implicitly on the premise that sexual responsiveness and the functioning of the reproductive system should be related, either because they both involve pelvic organ systems or because they are both important aspects of a larger phenomenon called femininity. It is a plausible line of thought, but when one looks at the available scientific information dealing with this issue, one finds little that is convincing. There is no solid support for the view that amount of menstrual pain and discomfort and degree of menstrual irregularity are related to sexual responsiveness. Interestingly, it is also true that no convincing evidence can be mustered that menstrual discomfort is greater in women who are seriously maladjusted than in those without psychiatric symptomatology.

One is left with the overall impression that it would be well to be sceptical of anyone who forcefully claims that a woman who has difficulties in being sexually responsive will be particularly susceptible to menstrual, pregnancy, and other pelvic malfunctions. An intriguing thing that was discovered in the course of analysing various findings pertaining to pregnancy was that the pregnant woman is probably no more psychologically disturbed that the nonpregnant woman. Although some have urged that pregnancy is a time of profound and unusual turmoil for the average woman, one finds upon close examination that even when empirical studies underlie this view they have neglected to use adequate control groups. It is possible to find considerable anxiety and psychopathology in pregnant women, but just as much can probably be found in the nonpregnant. The pregnant woman may have different kinds of concerns than the nonpregnant, but it is doubtful that she has a greater total amount of disturbance. One should add that if pregnancy were as disturbing a process as some would have us believe, it is unlikely that pregnancy rates would be as high as they are. The fact is that the majority of women probably look forward eagerly to the child-bearing experience.

It is of further pertinence that I could detect few consistent differences between the psychological state of menstruating women and those not menstruating. Such findings suggest that women learn to adapt rather quickly to the demands associated with their reproductive functions. Both popularly and clinically it has been fashionable to portray the menstruating or pregnant woman as existing in a state of delicate balance, but this is not a reasonable stereotype. In fact, a function like menstruation seems to take on important femininity-defining significance and, in addition, may, because of its regular cyclic nature, introduce a stabilizing rhythm into the life of the average woman. It is true that clinicians not infrequently encounter women who complain about discomfort associated with various aspects of their reproductive systems, but they also encounter many who have discomfort in nonreproductive systems. The ratio of reproductive to nonreproductive complaints probably conforms to the ratio of the total anatomical size of the reproductive systems to that of the nonreproductive. Although certain of the physiological changes that occur in a woman's body are stressful, there is no reason to assume that they are, in any general sense, seriously threatening. A person is capable of adapting well to profound alterations in his body, especially if the adaptation occurs over a relatively long period of time. It is too easily overlooked that even those who have gross body deformities and serious physiological difficulties usually learn to cope with them without persistent serious disturbance. The stress arising from menstruation and pregnancy is almost certainly considerably less than that derived from such gross kinds of body difficulties. The major adaptation problem associated with pregnancy may actually be the abrupt change in state which occurs when the child is delivered. Suddenly, the average woman experiences a gross alteration in her appearance; she is no longer the container for her child; she no longer has the special status and privileges of the pregnant; and she is confronted with new arduous duties involved in the care of the newborn. All of this happens in just a matter of minutes and hours. There are few life changes of equal magnitude which are condensed into such a tiny time interval. Even if some of the alterations are perceived favourably, they are radically abrupt. This may contribute to the relatively high psychosis rate in post-partum women.

A final point pertinent to the matter of pregnancy is that fear of accidental pregnancy does not seem to play an appreciable part in inhibiting sexual responsiveness. There were no consistent correlations in our data between any of the indices of sexual responsiveness and self-reported fear of becoming pregnant. Of course, it must be kept in mind that this negative result was obtained with samples of middle-class women who were largely satisfied with their contraceptive procedures. In women who either had no contraception available or whose contraception was seriously inadequate, one might expect fear of pregnancy to intrude significantly and interfere with sexual arousal. However, even in this more extreme group one wonders how strong the impact of fear of accidental pregnancy would be once the arousal process had started. While it might affect intercourse rate, would it prevent orgasm once intercourse had begun? One reason for being sceptical about this point derives from a report by Gebhard, *et al.* (1958) that women who have had an abortion (to terminate an unwanted pregnancy) do not have lower orgasm rates during their first year of marriage than other comparable women. It might have been expected that such women would be unusually anxious about becoming accidentally pregnant and that this anxiety would somehow interfere with their enjoyment of sexual stimulation. In any case, as contraceptive technology continues to become more efficient, whatever role fear of accidental pregnancy has had in modifying sexual arousal should practically disappear.

Practical Implications

If one takes the liberty of projecting from the results and generalizations presented in this book, a number of practical implications can be derived. These implications are offered in a tentative way. They go beyond the actual facts and should be approached with caution.

Pathways to Sexual Adequacy

One of the prime deductions to be made from the findings is that there are many pathways open to a woman in the process of becoming a sexually adequate person. She need not grow up with any special set of traits in order to be sexually responsive. Likewise, she need not conform to any fixed stereotype of what is feminine. Perhaps even more importantly, her sexual responsiveness does not depend on her achieving a certain fixed amount of practice in dating or heterosexual contacts as she grows up. Many different kinds of women with many different kinds of dating patterns have been found to be equally orgasmic. An immediate implication of these findings is that parents, psychiatrists, and others who are involved in the guidance or treatment of girls should be modest in their assertions about how any specific girl needs to behave in order to grow up to be a sexually adequate person. Perhaps only the most extreme kinds of deviance in sexual behaviour should be viewed as indicating a 'defect' in sexual development. There would seem to be little rationale in assuming that the developing girl is headed for disaster in her future sex role simply because she is shy with boys or does not easily wear certain of the standard trappings of femininity. Of course, it is still possible that the girl who is troubled with shyness and difficulties in relating to male peers may be headed for other kinds of adjustment difficulties.

A condition which can be regarded as a signal for potential future sexual difficulties is the existence of distant, non-involved relationship with father. It will be recalled that it was found that if a woman perceives her father as not having invested serious interest in her she tends to experience orgasmic difficulties. Therefore, if a girl has a father who is absent from home for long periods of time or whose work absorbs too great a part of his energies or who is psychologically difficult to relate to because of his own symptomatology (for example, alcoholism), serious thought ought to be given to the impact it will have upon her future sexual adaptation. Perhaps with an awareness of such potential complications, special remedial measures might be undertaken.

Sex Education

There has been interminable debate about the role of formal sex education in the child's long-term sexual development. Also, there have been conflicting opinions about how important it is for the parents, as compared to other people, to supply the child with information about sexual matters. If one uses as a criterion the adult sexual adequacy of a woman, the overall scientific findings indicate that the nature of *formal* sex education is relatively unimportant. Neither in our studies nor in those of others (Terman, 1938, 1951) has a woman's ability to enjoy sexual intercourse turned out to be related to the manner in which she received her early sex education. It made no difference whether she obtained her information from her mother or books or friends or a formal course in school. This is not to argue against giving accurate sexual information to children. Such information could in many instances help to correct inaccurate concepts of sexuality and relieve the individual of the need to go through a lot of unnecessary anxiety-provoking trial-and-error learning on his own. That is, sex education would help to clarify *cognitively* the essential nature of the sexual act and its relationship to reproduction. The benefit would be informational, at an intellectual level.

It is doubtful that formal sex education does much in terms of the individual's 'emotional' sexual development. It will be recalled that in our data there were no consistent relationships between a woman's sexual responsiveness and her recall of how openly her parents talked about sex or were comfortable with nudity. This suggests that much of what parents do that is *directly* concerned with sexual matters may have little to do with how comfortable their children will eventually be with sexual excitement. One would speculate that this is so because there are so many different reasons why parents may be open and explicit or closed and non-communicative about sex. In some instances the difference may actually reflect a degree of comfort with sexuality, but in other instances, façade or compensatory behaviour is probably involved. A parent may be very 'open' about sexual matters simply because he has read a book which insists that it is important to do so. Or he may be 'open' about sex as a way of forcefully denying real anxiety and insecurity in this area. On the other hand, he may be 'closed' about sex not because he is specifically ashamed of it but rather because he is restrained in communicating about any matters with personal or intimate connotations. One gets the impression from the available data that the really important things that a girl learns about sex from her parents are only minimally contained in those communications and behaviours which are clearly 'about sex'. Probably much more is learned from those aspects of their behaviour indicating how much they are capable of intimacy, trust, and dependability.

Sexual Adequacy

Women have been the targets of many unreasonable ideas about how they should behave sexually. For centuries they have been educated to believe that they are sexually inferior to men. They have been told that they are only castrated versions of men and that they are not really as sensitive to sexual stimuli as men. Pseudoscientific pronouncements have been utilized to reinforce such beliefs. As already shown, the empirical findings have not supported assumptions about women being sexually defective. It is true that women are less consistently able to attain orgasm in heterosexual intercourse than men are. However, it is highly probable that this is a reflection of certain special kinds of fears about separation from love objects which are generated by the way in which girls are socialized in most cultures. One would expect the orgasm consistency differential between the sexes to diminish (as it may already show signs of doing in the Kinsey, *et al.* [1953] data) when the female role is less radically defined in terms of dependence and winning the love of a protector.

Women have for some time been led to believe that they are neurotic, unhealthy, and immature if they prefer clitoral to vaginal stimulation. Once again the empirical facts indicate how badly they have been misled. Women who favour direct clitoral stimulation are in no way unusually immature or maladjusted. It is obvious from both the quantitative and qualitative material we collected that each woman has fairly special patterns of preference about attaining arousal; and there is no basis for asserting that any one pattern is 'healthier' than another. Further, my data indicate that direct clitoral manipulation plays a far larger role in attaining orgasm than previously suspected. Only 20 per cent of a sample questioned indicated that they never require the assistance of a final 'push' from *direct* clitoral stimulation in order to attain orgasm while engaged in intercourse. 64 per cent of one sample indicated that if they had to choose between clitoral and vaginal stimulation, they would settle for the clitoral. One can only guess that the elaborate fictions invented by men about the superiority of the so-called vaginal orgasm reflects the fact that they themselves enjoy a sexual relationship with a woman more when the penis is vaginally inserted than when it is not. In any case, there is no longer any rational reason for burdening women with restrictions on what is the 'proper' way for them to reach orgasm in a relationship with a man.

Sex and 'Mental Health'

Until evidence to the contrary appears, it must be urged that those who make decisions about whether women are psychologically maladjusted and in need of treatment do not use sexual responsiveness as one of their criteria. The available findings simply do not indicate a convincing relationship between degree of psychological disturbance and almost any aspect of sexual behaviour. Obviously, this conclusion clashes with some of the major viewpoints prevailing among professionals who dispense psychotherapeutic treatment. However, it is now clearly necessary to articulate a challenge to those who use limited sexual responsiveness in a woman as a sign of poor 'mental health'. The accumulated empirical observations place the burden of proof upon them. This is not to argue that psychotherapeutic techniques may not help women with orgasmic difficulties, but only that such difficulties should be regarded as occurring within a limited region of the personality and need not be representative of the state of other personality regions.

Treatment of Orgasm Difficulties

What deductions can be made from the findings which might be helpful in assisting an adult woman who has difficulty in attaining orgasm? This is a complex question because there are so many different levels at which 'assistance' might be provided. It could be offered in relatively simplistic ways involving direct intervention in immediate family and living arrangements, at one extreme, and esoteric psychotherapeutic procedures, at the other extreme. One can only review some of the possibilities which take on pertinence in the light of the fact that orgasm difficulties were observed to be linked to concern about the instability or potential loss of love objects. It will remain for future work to define the utility of these possibilities.

1. At the simplest level, one might begin by determining whether the husband (or sex partner) of the woman with orgasmic problems engages in modes of behaviour which dramatize his lack of dependability. Is he away for long periods of time? Does he fluctuate markedly in his acceptance of his wife? Does he engage in manoeuvres which chronically intimate that he plans to separate if things are not done his way? It is conceivable that if such behaviour patterns were called to the husband's attention (for example, in the context of joint marital therapy) that sufficient change could be induced to relieve some of the wife's feelings that he is undependable. This, in turn, might sufficiently reduce her overall concern about potential object loss to help increase her ability to tolerate orgasmic excitement.

2. A second possible approach would be in terms of individual psychotherapeutic exploration which focused on issues of object loss. This would particularly involve an analysis of the woman's feelings and fantasies about the father, who, it will be recalled, seemed to play a selectively important role in those attitudes which inhibit orgasm. The essence of such psychotherapeutic work would be to make the woman aware of her original uncertainty about father's lack of dependability and to give her insight into her tendency to overgeneralize and apply what seemed to be true of the father to her current heterosexual transactions.

3. A third treatment alternative I would propose for consideration (and empirical evaluation) aims to cope directly with the perceptual 'fading' process which has been presumed to elicit orgasm inhibition in women who are particularly concerned about object loss. It was earlier theorized that when a woman is sensitive to object loss she finds a build-up of sexual excitement to be threatening because it is accompanied by diminished perceptual sensitivity and a retreat from what is 'out there', which results in a feeling of having a less secure perceptual hold on objects and therefore less actual attachment to them. The question arises whether the woman with orgasmic difficulties could be helped if she were made explicitly aware of the perceptual changes accompanying sexual excitement and also her interpretation of these

changes. If she could more directly face up to the perceptual 'fading' process and become aware of her irrational assumptions concerning its significance, she might learn to master its threatening implications. Indeed, if she could be assigned the task of repeatedly building up sexual excitement (for example, via masturbation) and studying the perceptual changes produced she might gradually become less sensitized to their impact – and so ultimately less likely to become inhibited as orgasm approaches.

Nonsexual Functions of Sex

There are hints here and there in my findings that sexual behaviour serves other needs than those which would be considered sexual in the strict sense of the term. For example, intercourse rates were found to be correlated with certain indices of narcissism. Further, masturbation frequency was found to be correlated not only with interest in novel experience but also with wishes having to do with demonstrating one's independence from the mother. Of course, many other theorists and clinicians have pointed out the nonsexual satisfactions or purposes that sexual behaviour may serve in the life of an individual. I would like to suggest that insufficient recognition has been given to nonsexual derivatives of various sexual behaviours. Actually, most persons probably tend to feel guilt or a sense of inappropriateness when they become aware of such nonsexual derivatives in their own lives. But one wonders whether discomfort of this sort might be partially dispelled if there were wider explicit recognition of the nonsexual functions of sex. The woman who gets the urge to masturbate because she has the desire to affirm again her independence of mother need not intrinsically have a greater sense of inappropriateness than she does when she eats to allay a *general* feeling of uneasiness or takes a shower to help her articulate her body boundaries. This statement is made, of course, entirely from a nonmoralistic perspective and would not apply within the context of religious beliefs which, because they define nonsexual uses of sex as immoral, produce guilt and discomfort.

Education

The more educated a woman is the less she typifies the usual stereotypes about femininity. It is a characteristic finding in studies which evaluate degree of femininity, as defined by interest patterns, that women with much education are 'less feminine' than those with limited education. A widely accepted belief is that a well-educated woman has somehow lost an important component of her womanhood. Education is thought to masculinize a woman and to diminish her likelihood of being passionate. It is an interesting commentary on the divergence between speculative assumptions and real fact that empirical studies have shown just the opposite to be true. As already described in detail, Kinsey, *et al.* (1953) discovered that orgasm consistency is positively related to amount of education Also, they reported that the difference between women with low and high amounts of education does not disappear even after many years of sexual practice in marital intercourse. Women have been misled concerning the impact that education might have upon them as sexual persons. They have been led to fear that the educational process would make them all 'brain' and diminish their body sexuality proportionately. One can only say that it is time to emancipate them from this belief by a straightforward reassurance that it is untrue. There are analogous beliefs to the effect that if women aspire to roles or types of work which are conventionally masculine they will somehow lose their sexuality. While no scientific information is available about whether women in more 'masculine' occupations are less sexually responsive than women in conventional sex status roles, one would doubt it in view of the writer's findings that measures of 'masculinity of interest' were unrelated to sex responsiveness indices. It is very unlikely that the housewife or the feminine looking model are more orgasmic than the woman engineer or taxi driver.

Sexual Practice Effects

Comment should be made about the practical implications of the relatively minimal role that sheer amount of sexual practice (as in marital intercourse) has been found to play in orgasm consistency. Years of marital intercourse seem to have rather unimpressive effects on orgasm attainment. It will be recalled, too, that measures of the elaborateness of the sexual stimulation delivered to women were found by me and also others (Kinsey, *et al.*, 1953) to be uncorrelated with sexual responsiveness. For example, I noted that the number of intercourse positions and length of foreplay had only chance correlations with orgasm consistency. A primary deduction to be made from such material is that the ability to be orgasmic cannot be learned by an adult woman in the way that she learns other motor skills. It is doubtful that she can really improve her orgasm capacity significantly by reading books on sexual technique or experimenting with a variety of stimulation procedures. Beyond a moderate level of knowledge concerning primary erogenous zones, the factors facilitating orgasmic arousal seem to be largely interpersonal, involving feelings of intimacy, closeness, and dependability. Women with orgasm difficulties probably try to convince themselves that if only they could master some new sexual technique all would be well. Or they may irrationally criticize their sex partners for not being sufficiently expert to stimulate them properly. In other words, the attainment of orgasm is too often perceived as a motor act which can be mastered in the same way as any muscular manoeuvre. For what it is worth, let me add that I found no significant correlations between orgasm consistency and amount of investment in athletic activities. It is doubtful that the ability to reach orgasm is any more a function of motor skill than is the ability to enjoy eating.

Pregnancy

Part of the folklore about female sexuality is that a woman does not reach genuine sexual maturity until she has had the experience of bearing a child. This concept has probably motivated many women with orgasm difficulties to become pregnant. Sherfey (1966) has even given the concept an apparent scientific basis by proposing that pregnancy, by increasing the vascularity of the pelvis, augments 'orgasmic competency'. She declares at one point (p. 90): 'Many women experience their first coital orgasm after their first pregnancy'. There were no indications in the writer's findings that women who had had one or more pregnancies were any more orgasmic than those who had never been pregnant. There were no differences between these categories either with respect to orgasm consistency or other measures of sexual responsiveness. One can imagine that bearing a child might in certain individual instances increase a woman's orgasmic consistency; but if so, I would attribute it to a sense of increased security about being part of a stable family group. That is, the birth of a child might signal to a woman that her marriage did, indeed, have permanence and that her husband could be counted on to maintain their liaison. However, it is also possible to imagine that the birth of a child would alienate a husband and cause the wife to feel more insecure about her marriage and her husband. This could conceivably eventuate in diminished orgasmic consistency. But, in general, I would maintain that it is unlikely that any one psychological or physiological event will drastically alter a woman's sexual responsiveness. It is unrealistic to advise a woman with an orgasm problem that if she would only become pregnant or find a new sex partner or shift from an 'outside' job to being a housewife that her ability to respond to orgasm would be significantly augmented. Such advice has no foundation in fact.

Final Comment

A mixture of fact and speculation has been presented. But an earnest effort has been made to distinguish the one from the other. We need to acknowledge frankly that our understanding of female sexuality remains at an elementary stage. Many more studies will have to be carried out before we accumulate a wide range of dependable knowledge concerning the nature of the female sexual experience. Meanwhile, it is advisable to be sceptical of any global or 'easy' formulations in this area. What else can one conclude in view of the fact that the validity of so many widely and long accepted concepts about sexuality seem now to be in question?

Epilogue

As I have had time to gain distance from the material presented in this book, I have become convinced that the preoccupation of Western culture with the nature of the female orgasm represents a puzzled concern about what should be the proper model of womanhood. I would speculate that our concern over the fact that so many women do not consistently reach orgasm reflects our underlying awareness that powerful anti-feminine directions in our culture make life inordinately difficult for many women. Indeed, our exaggerated, often unrealistic anxiety about the dire potentiality of other categories of female physiology (for example, menstruation) has a guilty quality. There are few aspects of modern women which have aroused as many nurturant efforts on her behalf as her reproductive system. The gynaecologist has been assigned an extremely onerous rescue role. It is my hunch that much of the anxiety which has been focused on the woman's reproductive system is a coded and condensed way of atoning for other unfair things that are generally done to her. But it is interesting that women too have been caught up by this attitude and have learned to view their own pelvic structures as fragile – proper target for feelings of uneasiness. In woman's 'acceptance' of the attitude she helps to maintain an indirect tension-relieving system which puts off more direct action with reference to the real issues involved.

The debate about whether all women should have orgasms and also whether there are proper or improper ways for them to achieve orgasmic excitement seems to mirror a longstanding ambivalence about what is a woman's proper role in a sexual transaction. To perceive her as one who should consistently reach orgasm is to define her as having equal rights with the male in the midst of their intimacy. A similar declaration of equality is implied in the assumption that there is no stigma in her preferring sexual stimulation to those parts of her body which are most arousing for her, rather than those which immediately bring the greatest pleasure to her male partner. It is apparent that our new preoccupation with the female orgasm is simply a statement that we are uneasy about the old definitions of male-female intimacy and are in the process of revising them.

The psychological factors – for example, fear of object loss – which our work suggests may interfere with orgasm attainment, in many women may exemplify at another level the general cultural feeling transmitted to women that her place is uncertain and that she survives only because the male protects her. The apparent importance of fear of object loss in inhibiting orgasm can probably be traced to the fact that the little girl gets innumerable messages which tell her that the female cannot survive as a single entity and is likely to get into serious trouble if not supported by a strong and capable male. It does not seem too radical to predict that when women are able to grow up in a cultural matrix in which they are less pressured to obedience by threats of potential desertion, the so-called orgasm problem will fade away. However, it is an interesting commentary on life's complexities that as women learn to adopt new basic orientations, some analogous to the masculine stance, they may develop other kinds of 'body problems' which currently plague men more than they do women. The body remains one of our prime locales for acting out attitudes and feelings which are too disapproved of or threatening to express publicly in words.

References

Ard, B. N., 'Sexual Behavior and Attitudes of Marital Partners', unpublished doctoral dissertation, University of Michigan, 1962.

Arlow, J. A., 'Masturbation and symptom formation', *Journal of the American Psychoanalytic Association*, 1953, 1, 45–58.

Bakker, C. B., and Dightman, C. R., 'Psychological factors in fertility control', *Fertility and Sterility*, 1964, 15, 559–67.

Bradford, Jean L., 'Sex differences in anxiety', unpublished doctoral dissertation, University of Minnesota, 1968.

Bronfenbrenner, U., 'Some familial antecedents of responsibility and leadership in adolescents'. In L. Petrullo and B. M. Bass (Eds.), *Leadership and Interpersonal Behavior*, New York, Holt, Rinehart, Winston, 1961, pp. 239–71.

Chesser, Eustace, *The sexual, marital and family relationships of the English woman*, New York, Roy Publishers, 1957.

Clausen, J., 'The Effects of Amphetamine and Barbiturates on Body Experience', presented at annual meeting of American Psychosomatic Society, Denver, Colorado, 1971.

Coppen, A., 'The prevalence of menstrual disorders in psychiatric patients', *British Journal of Psychiatry*, 1965, 111, 155–67.

Davis, Katharine B., *Factors in the Sex Life of Twenty-two Hundred Women*, New York, Harper and Bros., 1929.

Douvan, Elizabeth, and Adelson, J., *The adolescent experience*, New York, John Wiley & Sons, 1966.

Ellis, A., 'Guilt, shame, and frigidity', *Quarterly Review of Surgery, Obstetrics, and Gynecology*, 1959, 16, 259–61.

Fast, G. J., and Fisher, S., 'The role of body attitudes and acquiescence in epinephrine and placebo effects', *Psychosomatic Medicine*, 1971, 33, 63–84.

Fenichel, O., *The psychoanalytic theory of neurosis*, New York, W. W. Norton & Co., 1945.

Fish, Kathleen D., 'Paternal Availability, Family Role Structure, Maternal Employment, and Personality Development in Late Adolescent Females', unpublished doctoral dissertation, University of Massachusetts, 1969.

Fisher, S., *Body Consciousness: You Are What You Feel*, Englewood Cliffs, New Jersey, Prentice-Hall, 1973.

— *Body Experience in Fantasy and Behavior*, New York, Appleton-Century-Crofts, 1970.

— *The Female Orgasm: Psychology, Physiology, Fantasy*, New York, Basic Books, 1973.

Gebhard, P. H., Pomeroy, W. B., Martin, C. E., and Christenson, Cornelia V., *Pregnancy, birth and abortion*, New York, Harper & Bros., 1958.

Gleser, Goldine C., Gottschalk, L. A., and Springer, K. J. 'An Anxiety Scale Applicable to Verbal Samples', *Archives of General Psychiatry*, 1961, 5, 593–605.

Goshen-Gottstein, Esther R., 'Courtship, marriage and pregnancy in "Geula": A study of an ultra-orthodox Jerusalem group', *The Israel Annals of Psychiatry and Related Disciplines*, 1966, 4, 43–66.

Greenacre, Phyllis, 'Special Problems of Early Female Sexual Development' In H. M. Ruitenbeek (Ed.), *Psychoanalysis and Female Sexuality*, New Haven, Connecticut, College and University Press, 1966, pp. 140–60.

Kanin, E. J., and Howard, D. H., 'Postmarital consequences of Premarital Sex Adjustments', *American Sociological Review*, 1958, 23, 556–62.

Katcher, A., 'The discrimination of sex differences by young children', *Journal of Genetic Psychology*, 1955, 87, 131–43.

Katcher, A., and Levin, M., 'Children's Conceptions of Body Size', *Child Development*, 1955, 26, 103–10.

Keiser, S., 'Body ego during orgasm', *Psychoanalytic Quarterly*, 1952, 21, 153–66.

Kinsey, A. C., Pomeroy, W., Martin, C., and Gebhard, P., *Sexual behavior in the human female*, Philadelphia, Saunders, 1953.

Laing, R. D., *The Self and Others*, London, Tavistock Publications, 1959.

Landis, C., *Sex in development*, New York, Paul B. Hoeber, 1940.

Landis, C., Bolles, Marjorie M., and D'Esopo, D. A., 'Psychological and Physical Concomitants of Adjustment in Marriage', *Human Biology*, 1940, 12, 559–65.

Landis, J., Poffenberger, T., and Poffenberger, S., 'The Effects of First Pregnancy upon the Sexual Adjustment of 212 couples', *American Sociological Review*, 1950, 15, 767–72.

Lehfeldt, H., and Guze, H., 'Psychological factors in contraceptive failure', *Fertility and Sterility*, 1966, 17, 110.

Lewis. Selma A., 'Experimental induction of Castration Anxiety and Anxiety Over Loss of Love', unpublished doctoral dissertation, Yeshiva University, 1969.

Lowery, R. J., 'Male-female differences in attitudes toward death', unpublished doctoral dissertation, Brandeis University, 1965.

Manosevitz, M., and Lanyon, R. I., 'Fear Survey Schedule: A normative study', *Psychological Reports*, 1965, 17, 699–703.

Masters, R. E. L. [Ed.] *Sexual self-stimulation*, Los Angeles, California, Sherbourne Press, 1967.

Masters, W. H., and Johnson, Virginia E., *Human sexual response*, Boston, Little, Brown, 1966.

Melzner, R. J., and Golden, J. S., 'Psychological Factors Influencing Female Patients in the Selection of Contraceptive Devices, *Fertility and Sterility*, 1967, 18, 845–56.

Pfeiffer, E., Verwoerdt, A., and Wang, H., 'Sexual Behavior in Aged Men and Women. I. Observations on 254 community volunteers', *Archives of General Psychiatry*, 1968, 19, 753–8.

Pohlman, E., *The psychology of birth planning*, Cambridge, Massachusetts, Schenkman Publishing, 1969.

Pomeroy, W. B., 'Some aspects of prostitution', *Journal of Sex Research*, 1965, 1, 177–87.

Rainwater, L., *Family design. Marital Sexuality, Family Size, and Contraception*, Chicago, Illinois, Aldine Publishing, 1965.

Rodgers, D. A., and Ziegler, F. J., 'Changes in Sexual Behavior Consequent to Use of Noncoital Procedures of Contraception', *Psychosomatic Medicine*, 1968, 30, 495–505.

Rodgers, D. A., Ziegler, F. J., Prentiss, R. J., and Martin, P. L., 'Comparisons of Nine Contraceptive Procedures by Couples Changing to Vasectomy or Ovulation Suppression Medication', *Journal of Sex Research*, 1965, 1, 87–96.

Roe, Anne, and Siegelman, L., 'A Parent-Child Relations Questionnaire', *Child Development*, 1963, 34, 355–69.

Schaefer, Leah C., 'Sexual Experiences and Reactions of a Group of 30 Women As Told to a Female Psychotherapist', unpublished doctoral dissertation, Columbia University, 1964.

Schofield, M., *The Sexual Behaviour of Young People*, Boston, Little, Brown, 1965.

Sherfey, Mary J., 'The Evolution and Nature of Female Sexuality in Relation to Psychoanalytic Theory', *Journal of the American Psychoanalytic Association*, 1966, 14, 28–128.

Shope, D. F., 'A Comparison of Selected College Females on Sexual

Responsiveness and Nonresponsiveness', unpublished doctoral dissertation, Pennsylvania State University, 1966.

Sigusch, V., Schmidt, G., Reinfeld, A., and Wiedemann-Sutor, I., 'Psychosexual Stimulation: Sex Differences', *Journal of Sex Research*, 1970, 6, 10–24.

Terman, L. M., *Psychological Factors in Marital Happiness*, New York, McGraw-Hill, 1938.

Terman, L. M., *Studies in personality*, New York, McGraw-Hill, 1942.

Terman, L. M., 'Correlates of Orgasm Adequacy in a Group of 556 Wives', *Journal of Psychology*, 1951, 32, 115–72.

Thomason, G. B., 'Differential Non-sexual and Sexual Behavior in the Marital Adjustment of Penn State Alumni', unpublished doctoral dissertation, Pennsylvania State College, 1951.

Udry, J. R., and Morris, Naomi M., 'A Method for Validation of Reported Sexual Data, *Journal of Marriage and The Family*, 1967, 29, 442–6.

Wineman, Eugenia W., 'Some Psychophysiological Correlates of the Human Menstrual Cycle', unpublished doctoral dissertation, University of California, Los Angeles, 1967.

Winokur, G. (Ed.), *Determinants of Human Sexual Behavior*, Springfield, Illinois, Charles C. Thomas, 1963.

Winokur, G., Guze, S. B., and Pfeiffer, E., 'Developmental and Sexual Factors in Women: A Comparison Between Control, Neurotic and Psychotic Groups', *American Journal of Psychiatry*, 1958–59, 115, 1097–1100.

The Sexual Behaviour of Young People

Michael Schofield

This report sets out to supply facts in an area in which sensation has tended to flourish. Michael Schofield's findings are based on the results of some 2,000 interviews held in England with young people between the ages of thirteen and nineteen.

The first fact to emerge is that sexual promiscuity, though it certainly exists, is not a prominent feature of teenage behaviour. Consequently the risk of venereal disease among the young is not high: infections, it is true, have increased lately, but less in this age-group than in others. Illegitimacy, according to this report, presents a graver problem: of every three girls who have premarital sexual intercourse, one can expect to become pregnant.

Scare reports about immorality and disease have raised a cry for improved sex education. Statistics given in this book certainly suggest that the majority of adolescents still receive little or no guidance from parents or teachers. The facts of contraception and venereal disease are almost outside their ken.

Michael Schofield's meticulous and balanced survey provides the kind of evidence (and the stimulus) needed for framing a sound plan of education and advice about sex for the young.

Child Care and the Growth of Love

John Bowlby

In 1951, under the auspices of the World Health Organization, Dr John Bowlby wrote a report on *Maternal Care and Mental Health* which collated expert world opinion on the subject and the issues arising from it – the prevention of juvenile and adult delinquency, the problem of the 'unwanted child', the training of women for motherhood, and the best ways of supplying the needs of children deprived of their natural mothers. This Pelican is a summary of Dr Bowlby's report, freed from many of its technicalities and prepared for the general reader.

This revised edition contains chapters based on an article by Dr Mary Salter Ainsworth, written in 1962 also for the World Health Organization when it once again made an important study of child care.

'It is a convenient and scholarly summary of evidence of the effects upon children of lack of personal attention, and it presents to administrators, social workers, teachers and doctors a reminder of the significance of the family' – *The Times*

Marital Breakdown

J. Dominian

A marriage collapses. Psychology, sociology, and medicine may say one thing: religion and law pronounce another. In this study, probably for the first time, a psychiatrist has made an unbiased attempt to bring together these different viewpoints. How do men and women select their partners? asks Dr Dominian. And what are the factors that break a marriage up – sex, money, housing, parents and families, mental illness, or the inability to give and take emotionally? Do such influences as age or premarital pregnancy count?

The author makes no inspired guesses in answering these questions and is chary of ready-made solutions. Proceeding from the latest research he simply indicates the places where a deeper insight can help marriage counsellors and others to reconcile the parties and avoid breakdown. And he proposes ways in which the secular approach to divorce and the traditional Christian attitude might be harmonized.

From Woman to Woman

A gynaecologist answers questions about you and your body

Lucienne Lanson

At last, clear, accurate and sympathetic information from a gynaecologist – speaking woman to woman – in a book that will enable every woman to understand the workings of her own body and to discuss any treatment of it intelligently with her own doctor or gynaecologist.

Completely up-to-date, detailed, and authoritative, this book encompasses not only such common areas of concern as the gynaecological examination, irregular periods, menstrual cramps, fertility, and problems of the menopause – all considered from a psychological as well as a physical point of view in easy-to-follow question-and-answer form – but far more.

Here at last is guidance that combines the knowledge and experience of a practising gynaecologist with a woman's direct understanding of the way women feel about the female aspects of their bodies and the kinds of medical attention available to them. *From Woman to Woman* takes the frightening mystery out of the whole subject of gynaecology.